Christian Kids Explore Chemistry

Christian Kids Explore Chemistry

**Robert W. Ridlon, Jr.
Elizabeth J. Ridlon**

Dover, DE

Christian Kids Explore Chemistry
by Robert W. Ridlon, Jr. and Elizabeth J. Ridlon
A part of the Christian Kids Explore series

Published by Bright Ideas Press
P.O. Box 333, Cheswold, DE 19936
www.BrightIdeasPress.com

© 2005 by Bright Ideas Press. Printed and bound in the United States of America. All rights reserved. This book may not be duplicated in any way without the express written permission of the publisher, except in the form of brief excerpts or quotations for the purpose of review. Permission is granted to photocopy student activity sheets and other reproducibles for your own student, co-op, or classroom only. Not intended to be copied for an entire school. Making copies of this book, for any purpose other than stipulated, is a violation of the United States copyright laws.

Cover illustration by David Taylor
Interior illustrations by Laura Cochran

Cover and interior design by Pneuma Books, LLC
visit www.pneumabooks.com for more information.

Library of Congress Cataloging-in-Publication Data

Ridlon, Robert W.
  Christian kids explore chemistry / Robert W. Ridlon, Jr., Elizabeth J. Ridlon. — 1st ed.
       p. cm. — (Christian kids explore)
  Includes index.
  ISBN-13: 978-1-892427-18-2 (softcover : alk. paper)
  ISBN-10: 1-892427-18-4 (softcover : alk. paper)
 1. Chemistry—Experiments. 2. Chemistry--Study and teaching (Elementary)—Activity programs. 3. Christian education—Activity programs. I. Ridlon, Elizabeth J. II. Title. III. Series.

QD43.R53 2005
372.35--dc22

LCCN: 2005011911

10 09 08 07

6 5 4 3 2

This book is dedicated to the brave military men and women who defend our freedom around the world.

"Through God we shall do valiantly, and it is He who will tread down our adversaries."
~ Psalm 60:12

TABLE OF CONTENTS

A Note From the Author..xv

How to Use This Book..xix

Unit One:
The Basics of Chemistry 1

○ Lesson 1: Introduction to Chemistry.................................. 5
Hands-On: Discovering Matter 8

○ Lesson 2: Chemistry Tools 13
Hands-On: Measuring 16

○ Lesson 3: Matter 21
Hands-On: Separating Compounds by Filtration 24

○ Lesson 4: Elements 29
Hands-On: Making Element Cards 32

○ Lesson 5: Mixtures and Compounds 37
Hands-On: Examining Mixtures and Compounds 40

○ Unit One Wrap-Up 45

Unit Two:
Atoms and Molecules 51

Lesson 6: Atoms 55
Hands-On: Building Atomic Models 58

Lesson 7: Atomic Number 63
Hands-On: Labeling the Subatomic Particles 65

Lesson 8: Atomic Mass 69
Hands-On: Catch Up on Element Cards 72

Lesson 9: Periodic Table 75
Hands-On: Using the Periodic Table 79

Lesson 10: Molecules 83
Hands-On: Building Molecular Models 85

Unit 2 Wrap-Up 89

Unit Three:
The Nature of Chemistry 95

Lesson 11: Chemical Bonds 99
Hands-On: Filtering Salt Water 101

Lesson 12: More Chemical Bonds 107
Hands-On: Breaking Covalent Bonds 109

Lesson 13: Formulas 113
Hands-On: Catch Up on Element Cards 115

Lesson 14: Naming Compounds 119
Hands-On: Naming Compounds 121

Table of Contents

- **Lesson 15: Reactions** 125
  - Hands-On: Chemical Reaction 128

- **Lesson 16: Acids** 131
  - Hands-On: Hunting for Acids 133

- **Lesson 17: Bases** 137
  - Hands-On: Hunting for Bases 139

- **Lesson 18: Salts** 143
  - Hands-On: Dissolving Calcium Carbonate with Acid 145

- **Unit Three Wrap-Up** 149

Unit Four:
States of Matter 157

- **Lesson 19: Solids and Liquids** 161
  - Hands-On: Determining the Volume of a Solid 164

- **Lesson 20: Gases** 169
  - Hands-On: Catch Up on Element Cards 171

- **Lesson 21: Gas Laws** 175
  - Hands-On: Testing Charles's Gas Law 177

- **Lesson 22: State Change** 181
  - Hands-On: Evaluating the Freezing Point of NaCl in Water 184

- **Lesson 23: Solutions** 189
  - Hands-On: Preparing a Saturated Solution 191

- **Unit Four Wrap-Up** 197

Unit Five
Organic Chemistry 203

Lesson 24: Hydrocarbons 207
Hands-On: Floating Hydrocarbons 211

Lesson 25: Alkanes 215
Hands-On: Building an Alkane Hydrocarbon Model 217

Lesson 26: Alkenes 221
Hands-On: Building an Alkene Hydrocarbon Model 223

Lesson 27: Alkynes 227
Hands-On: Building an Alkyne Hydrocarbon Model 229

Lesson 28: AlcOHols 233
Hands-On: Evaluating the Freezing Point of Alcohol 235

Lesson 29: Esters 241
Hands-On: The Crayon as a Hydrocarbon Product 243

Lesson 30: Biochemistry 247
Hands-On: Evaluating Products for Macromolecules 250

Unit Five Wrap-Up 255

Glossary 261

Coloring Pages 269

Appendix A
Element Tables 281

Appendix B
Resource List 287

Appendix C
For Further Biographical Study 307

Answer Key: Unit One Wrap-Up 315

Answer Key: Unit Two Wrap-Up 321

Answer Key: Unit Three Wrap-Up 327

Answer Key: Unit Four Wrap-Up 335

Answer Key: Unit Five Wrap-Up 344

Index 347

About the Authors 357

Acknowledgments

We are grateful foremost to God who perfectly provides for our every need — especially by providing Jesus as our savior.

Next, to our parents, Robert and Darlene Ridlon and James and Carolyn Woolf, who encouraged and nurtured us to be good citizens among God's creation.

To our teachers (the good ones) who were both a source of inspiration and revelation as we sought to find our way as explorers in an unknown world.

To our church families who throughout the years have reflected God's love, shining a light on our path and warming our hearts.

To the Christian leaders who have set examples for us to follow and encouraged us as fellow soldiers of the cross.

Special thanks to Stephanie Redmond and Maggie Hogan for introducing us to the Christian Kids Explore series and letting us be participants.

A Note from the Author

Exploring chemistry can be an exciting adventure — just like exploring some mysterious ancient ruins. Chemistry, like other sciences, gives us a glimpse into the wonders of God's creation.

Don't Be Afraid!

Chemistry has had a reputation of being an almost out-of-reach activity only for a few "special" people. Much of that reputation comes from the unfamiliar words, rules, tools, and procedures that define it. Although chemistry isn't simple, we believe that it can be made easy to understand.

Don't Be Intimidated!

We learn new and complicated things every day — from computer programs and games to new moves in a sport to a new song on a musical instrument. We are always learning. Chemistry is no different — it takes time and perseverance.

Chemistry Can Be Fun and Exciting!

Just like getting to know music, sports, or even a new board game, we will learn some terms, some notations, and some rules. Each of our lessons develops a progressive understanding of chemistry that will build confidence. Kids and parents can explore and develop a firm and lasting foundation for the future.

We hope you will be encouraged by these words from Proverbs: "Trust in the Lord with all your heart and lean not on your own understanding; in all your ways acknowledge him and he will make your paths straight" (Prov. 3:5-6).

Robert W. Ridlon, Jr.
Elizabeth J. Ridlon

HOW TO USE THIS BOOK

This book contains 30 lessons. Each lesson is designed to be completed in one week. If you teach science twice weekly, allow for about 60 to 90 minutes each day.

Some of the lessons may seem a little more challenging than others. Less advanced students may have some difficulty with fully comprehending all the material in these few challenging lessons. Don't worry! It is quite satisfactory if the student can just learn the foundational concepts that are represented by the Review It questions at the end of the lesson. Don't rush! You may have to read the lesson slowly and more than once. If some words are too difficult, use a dictionary or other source to help clarify meanings. This work will pay off when it's time for the upper level classes or when other challenges come along that require perseverance.

Step by Step
Lesson Activities

The following activities are included in each lesson and unit:

Additional Notes

Preparation

The 30 lessons are divided into five units. The book begins with some overview lessons in the first unit and then presents the components and behavior of chemistry in the next three units. The last unit, organic chemistry, explores a type of chemistry that is concerned with carbon compounds.

Each unit begins with a short note about the material covered in the unit lessons and a list of unit objectives, vocabulary words, and necessary materials. You may want to write the unit objectives on a piece of paper and keep it handy. Referring to the objectives will help give you confidence that the student is getting something from the material.

Teaching Time

Each lesson presents a topic that builds an understanding of chemistry layer by layer. Older or more advanced students can read the lesson material themselves. For very young or less advanced students, it is a good idea to read the lesson in advance and then explain it at their level. The student should be on the lookout for the vocabulary words that were identified in the unit introduction. Also, encourage the student to take a few notes to help them remember important ideas.

Review It

Do the review exercises. After the teaching time, each lesson has five Review It fill-in-the-blank exercises. The key to ensuring the student is ready for the upcoming hands-on activity and the next lesson is the successful completion of the fill-in-the-blank exercises. These are almost always exact quotes from the lesson and the answers are unambiguous. Once these are answered correctly, you should be confident that some important principles of chemistry have been learned.

Hands-On Time

This is the fun stuff. Each lesson ends with a hands-on activity. These activities have a two-fold purpose: they reinforce some of the concepts from the lessons, and they will be a chance for a student to experience being a chemist.

Coloring Pages

There is one coloring page per unit and all of these, plus a few extra, are found after the glossary. These may be photocopied. Children of all ages will enjoy these beautiful drawings.

Think about It

This is a critical thinking exercise regarding the results of the hands-on activity. It isn't absolutely necessary to do, but it offers a more advanced student the opportunity to respond to some questions that require some creative thought. This also might be an alternative to the coloring page for the older student.

Unit Wrap-Up

At the end of each unit, there is an opportunity for the student to show what they have learned. The questions are in a multiple-choice format and are taken almost exactly from the lesson review exercises. So, a great way to prepare is to go over each review exercise for the lessons in that unit. The answer key for the Unit Wrap-Ups start on page 311.

What's Important?
Building a Fountain

The important thing to keep in mind is that God is at the center of everything — including the study of chemistry. The more advanced or older student may get more chemistry from the book

Additional Notes

Additional Notes

than a younger or less advanced student. It might be good to repeat this course every other year. Build a foundation. Things learned early will last a lifetime. Do your best— and have fun and learn!

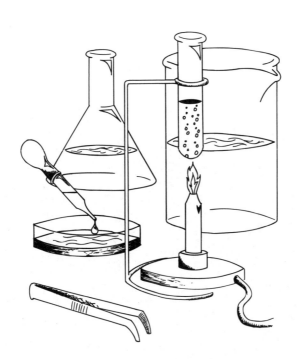

Unit One
The Basics of Chemistry

In this unit we will begin exploring the world of chemistry and see just how wonderfully God has made the universe and every living thing. Studying chemistry, like other sciences, is a way to appreciate creation more deeply and examine the beauty of all that God has made.

The universe was created by God and is made up of matter and energy that can be studied. Everything that we see or touch is matter. Chemistry shows us God's laws about how that matter behaves and helps us to take better care of our resources. We will start by defining chemistry and looking at the tools of the chemist.

Additional Notes

Upon completing Unit One, the student should understand:

- The basic objectives of chemistry
- The chemistry laboratory and tools of the chemist
- The definition of matter
- The composition of matter

Unit One Vocabulary Words

- chemistry
- chemist
- matter
- biology
- biochemistry
- organic chemistry
- inorganic chemistry
- lab coat
- safety glasses
- apparatus
- interpolate
- atoms
- energy
- physics
- states
- physical properties
- chemical properties
- element
- compound
- mixtures

Unit One: The Basics of Chemistry

Materials Needed for This Unit

- cereal box
- cleaning agent (such as window cleaner or general purpose cleaner)
- shampoo
- ordinary household measuring cup marked in metric units (milliliters) or a graduated cylinder if available
- small juice glass or cup
- notebook
- pencil
- salt (regular table salt)
- cup of fine sand
- bowl (like a cereal bowl)
- ordinary coffee filter
- funnel
- clear 16-ounce glass jar or drinking glass
- aluminum pie pan
- water
- measuring cup
- 100 3x5 lined index cards
- cooking oil
- sugar
- mustard
- six small bowls (like cereal bowls)
- paper adhesive labels
- clear 16-ounce glass jar or drinking glass
- safety glasses and smock

Additional Notes

Lesson 1
INTRODUCTION TO CHEMISTRY

Teaching Time:
What Is Chemistry?

What do you think of when someone says the word *chemistry*? Do you think about test tubes and glass containers filled with mysterious-looking yellow-green liquid? Do you think of jars of white powder? Maybe you think of a scientist wearing a white lab coat, mixing things together, and watching as the mixture bubbles and rumbles. It is true that chemists usually wear lab coats and often use various white, powder solids and colorful liquids. However, chemists also study substances that are familiar to us such as gold, silver, salt, water, and even food items, such as sugars and fats.

So, just what is chemistry anyway? **Chemistry** is the structured and formal study of matter, how it can change, and how it reacts with other matter. A **chemist** is a specially trained scientist studies and works with matter. The word **matter** is used to mean anything that takes up or occupies space. A few examples of matter include dirt, sand, water, metals, rocks, salt, and wood. There are many other examples. Even the air we breathe is matter.

➡ **Name It!**
<u>chemistry</u>
The structured and formal study of matter, how it can change, and how it reacts with other matter.

<u>chemist</u>
A specially trained scientist who studies and works with matter.

<u>matter</u>
Anything that takes up or occupies space.

➡ Name It!

biology
The study of living things.

biochemistry
The study of the matter of living things.

organic chemistry
The study of matter that contains a substance called carbon.

carbon
The main ingredient in the fuels and oil used in our cars and aircraft. It is also part of the clothes we wear and the food we eat, one of the main ingredients for life itself and an essential ingredient for parts of our bodies and how we function.

inorganic chemistry
The study of matter that does not contain any carbon.

Living things (such as animals, plants, tiny bacteria, and really tiny viruses) are made up of matter also. **Biology** is the study of living things, and chemistry has an important role in biology. When chemists study the matter of living things, it is called **biochemistry**. Another very important type of chemistry, called **organic chemistry**, works with matter that contains a substance called carbon. **Carbon** is the main ingredient in the fuels and oil used in our cars and aircraft. It is also part of the clothes we wear and the food we eat. Did you know that a diamond is made of carbon? Carbon is also one of the main ingredients for life itself and an essential ingredient for parts of our bodies and how we function. **Inorganic chemistry** is the study of matter that does not contain any carbon. This includes substances like pure metals, salts, acids, and bases.

But chemistry is more than studying; it has many practical uses. Medical doctors, pharmacists, geologists, archaeologists, farmers, builders, and even cooks benefit from the knowledge and use of chemistry. It is the science of chemistry that gives us ways to make new materials or products that will help us in everyday life. Chemistry also provides the building blocks for medicines used to cure sicknesses like colds and flu or even more serious diseases like cancer and heart disease.

In our beginning study of chemistry we will be looking more closely at the different types of chemicals, how they react together, and what makes them unique. By learning about chemistry, we can better appreciate the created world. It is important to remember that when we study chemistry, we are really looking at God's creation. Chemists can see what matter is made of and how that matter reacts with other matter. The way matter behaves isn't an invention of the chemist — it is a creation of God. Remember, Genesis 1 tells us about the creation of the world, including the creation of matter.

God created the very first chemicals. He created the order of the entire universe, which includes the properties of all the chemicals. He created each and every living thing, which are made up of those chemicals. Most importantly, He made each one of us in

Lesson 1: Introduction to Chemistry

a special way. That means we are more than just chemicals — we have a spirit that can relate to God as our Creator.

In our study of chemistry, we will see the beauty of God's created world in the structure of the matter that is our world. In studying chemistry, we can see the work and thoughtfulness and intelligence of God.

Review It 5/11/10

1. Chemistry is the structured and formal study of _matter_.

2. A _chemist_ is a specially trained scientist who studies and works with matter.

3. God _created_ the very first chemicals, and He created the order of the entire universe.

4. Organic chemistry is the study of matter that contains a substance called _carbon_.

5. When chemists study the matter of living things, it is called _biochemistry_.

Additional Notes

Hands-On:
Discovering Matter

You may not realize it, but one place we see lots of chemistry is in our homes. Besides the obvious matter that exists all around us, there are also some great examples of chemical substances. Chemistry has a great impact on our daily lives. It's surprising just how many chemical products we have around us. Fortunately, there are labels on things that allow us to view their contents and see just what chemicals there are inside. In this first Hands-On, we will examine the labels on three products and then list their ingredients.

Equipment Needed

- cereal box
- cleaning agent (such as window cleaner or general purpose cleaner)
- shampoo

Activity

1. Choose one product in each of the three categories listed in the chart that follows.
2. Write the product name in the space provided at the top of the chart.
3. List the ingredients for each product in the chart.
4. See the example in the first column.

(Note: Some of the ingredients may be unfamiliar and may even seem like impossible words to pronounce, but this will help you

Lesson 1: Introduction to Chemistry

Soft Drink	Cereal	Cleaning Agent	Shampoo
Name: Coke	Name: Raisin Bran	Name: Window	Name: Water
Carbonated water	W.G. Wheat	Soap	Sodium Laureth Sul.
Sucrose	Raisin	Water	Cocamidopropyl
Caramel color	W. Bran	Vinegar	Ammonium Chloride
Phosphoric acid	Sugar		Imidazolidinyl
Natural flavors	H.F.C.s		DMDM Hydantoin
Caffeine	Salt Barley		Fragrance
			Quaterium
			Tetrasodium

understand that the things that seem common to our lives may actually be complicated chemicals.)

Additional Notes

Think about It

1. Had you ever heard of any of the ingredients before? Which ones?

   Salt Raisin Soap Sugar Water

Scripture
In the beginning God created the heavens and the earth. (Genesis 1:1)

Discovery Zone
Did you know that butter floats? Try it! Put a spoonful of butter in a glass of water and see what happens. We will find out why in lesson 24.

2. Which products had the most ingredients?

   shampoo

3. Do you think the ingredients were listed in a particular order?

   yes and no

4. Were there any ingredients in more than one product? Which ones?

   water

Done with with

Lesson 2

CHEMISTRY TOOLS

Teaching Time:
Test Tubes and Laboratories

Chemistry is usually studied in a laboratory. (You can call it a lab for short.) A laboratory is a place where chemicals are kept and where experiments and chemical reactions can occur safely. Sometimes the chemicals are poisonous or the reactions may produce substances that are poisonous. Sometimes chemical reactions can be violent and explosive. For that reason, chemical laboratories have specialized equipment and ways of doing things that prevent unnecessary danger. The laboratory also contains different types of equipment that are used to look at, test, and make chemical materials. In this lesson, we will look at some of the most common types of chemistry equipment and learn about basic laboratory procedures.

➲ **Name It!**

lab coat
A smock or shirt that protects a chemist's clothing from chemicals and even water. It also has some pockets to hold a pencil and safety glasses.

safety glasses
Glasses that protect a chemist's eyes during experiments.

apparatus
The equipment that a chemist uses, including containers, funnels, and tubing.

In the Laboratory

As we explore chemistry in this book, we won't be doing any dangerous experiments and we won't be using any dangerous chemicals. However, scientists are always careful, and we will be too. We will learn the proper ways to handle chemicals and equipment in any situation. In our study of chemistry, we will be doing hands-on activities that sometimes use a few common chemicals. These activities (labs) will involve safe reactions and safe substances to demonstrate some really cool chemistry.

We know that football players, pilots, or scuba divers always wear special clothing and equipment when they are doing their activities. A good chemist should also wear the right equipment when working in the lab. This includes two main items: a lab coat, or smock, and safety glasses. **The lab coat** protects our clothing from getting chemicals or even just water on them. It also has some pockets that provide a handy place for a pencil and safety glasses. Lab coats, in any size, don't cost very much. However, making a lab coat from a large old shirt can be just as good. **Safety glasses** are very important for protecting our eyes. Prescription eyeglasses work just fine; otherwise it is necessary to buy some safety glasses. They can be found at just about any hardware store for a few dollars. Both the lab coat and safety glasses can be worn when working in the lab and will be recommended in the instructions for certain hands-on activities.

A place with running water should be the laboratory for the hands-on activities. The kitchen and kitchen table are good since we won't be working with any poison or other dangerous chemicals. Normally, a laboratory has lots of different types of apparatus. **Apparatus** is the word for the equipment that a chemist uses, including containers, funnels, and tubing. These items are called glassware (although today, many of these items can be made of plastic). These apparatus are used for mixing, heating, observing, moving, pouring, and the other activities necessary for chemistry. The chemistry lab may also have other apparatus including many types of

5/27/10

Lesson 2: Chemistry Tools   15

special electronic equipment that are useful in figuring out what's in various substances. Finally, the chemistry lab will have a lot of different chemicals available depending on what the chemist needs. Let's take a closer look at some of the basic tools or apparatus of the chemist.

Review It
Label each piece of chemistry lab apparatus.

1. _test tube_

2. _erlenmeyer flask_

3. _beaker_

4. _glass tubing_

➡ **Name It!**

test tube
A glass cylinder with an opening at the top. This is used to hold and mix small amounts of chemicals.

Erlenmeyer flask
A special flask or container used to collect, hold, and mix chemicals.

beaker
Shaped similar to a drinking glass, it holds liquids, can be heated, allows for measuring, and has a spout for pouring.

glass tubing
Connects the different kinds of glassware together so liquids and gases can go from one container to another.

➔ **Name it!**

funnel
Allows for the easy collection of liquids poured from a container and then passes some of the liquid through to a container with a smaller top opening.

graduated cylinder
A long cylinder similar to a kitchen measuring cup but more accurate. It has marks along its side for measuring the liquid.

pipette
A long glass tube that works just like an eyedropper. It is used to pick up small amounts of liquid to move it from one container to another.

interpolate
To estimate a measurement

5. Funnel

Hands-On:
Measuring

One of a chemist's most important processes is measuring. Sometimes this requires the use of special instruments or machines. Sometimes it involves reading a thermometer or measuring using the laboratory glassware. In this Hands-On, we are going to measure the volume of a liquid and learn about reading a measuring device. We will also think about good laboratory methods. In this activity, we will measure a sample of water and determine the volume — in other words, the amount of water in our sample. Since we don't know the volume yet, we say that it is unknown.

Although precision lab apparatus allows very accurate measurement, sometimes we may have to read between the lines in order to get measurements. For example, let's say our measuring device (such as a measuring cup) has markings of 100, 200, 300, 400, and 500 milliliters. When measuring a liquid sample, we might find that the sample fills the measuring cup between the 200-milliliter line and the 230-milliliter line. In such a case, it is necessary to interpolate the reading. **Interpolate** means to make a good guess at what the reading would be if the measuring device had a mark at that very place where the sample level is. In this case, if the level is halfway, we could say the volume of the sample is 225 milliliters. If the level is between the 250 and the 260-milliliter line, we might be able to say the volume is about 255 milliliters. The best option, of course, is to use equipment

Lesson 2: Chemistry Tools

that allows us to measure accurately. For this Hands-On, we can use an ordinary measuring cup.

Equipment Needed

- ordinary household measuring cup that is marked in metric units (milliliters) or a graduated cylinder, if available
- small juice glass or cup
- notebook

Activity

Measurement	Water Amount	Notes
1		
2		
3		

1. Fill an ordinary juice glass with water.

2. Transfer the water from the juice glass into the measuring cup.

3. Look where the top of the water (the water line) meets the nearest mark on the measuring cup and write down the reading in the space below in milliliters. This represents the volume of water that was in the juice glass.

4. Pour the water back into the juice glass.

→ **Name It!**

thermometer
Temperature is important when chemicals react. The thermometer measures critical temperatures of the chemicals during experiments.

balance
Similar to a scale at the grocery store used to weigh fruits and vegetables. It is for measuring quantities of chemical substances.

Scripture
For we are God's workmanship, created in Christ Jesus to do good works, which God prepared in advance for us to do. (Ephesians 2:10)

Discovery Zone
The first perfect A chemistry student at Indiana University-South Bend was homeschooled in junior high. He graduated from college at age 16.

5. For a second time, pour the water from the juice glass into the measuring cup and record the measurement again.

6. Pour the water back into the juice glass.

7. For a third time, pour the water from the juice glass into the measuring cup and record the measurement.

Think about It

1. Was there any difference in the three readings? Did you expect any differences?

   _____

   _____

2. Look at the juice glass. Is there any water left in the bottom? Could that have made a difference in the readings?

   _____

   _____

3. Did you need to interpolate any of the readings?

   _____

   _____

4. What can you learn from this Hands-On?

   _____

   _____

Lesson 3

MATTER

Teaching Time:
Does Matter Matter?

Since chemistry is the study of matter, we need to begin by learning what matter is and the kinds of things we can study about it. An easy way to recognize **matter** is that it has weight and takes up space. That means everything we can see or touch is matter. Even some things you can't see, such as air, are matter. All matter is made up of small units called **atoms**.

An atom is so tiny that you cannot see it with your eye or even with a regular microscope, and it would seem to be weightless. However, each individual atom does have weight. Besides matter, what else could there be? How about light, electricity, or heat? These are examples of **energy**. Everything in this physical world can be placed in either of two categories: matter or energy. A chemical reaction is something that takes place between one type of matter and another. Energy is both used and produced in reactions. **Physics** is the scientific study of both matter and energy in great detail.

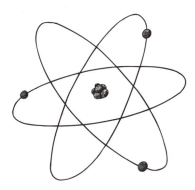

➲ Name It!

matter
Anything that has weight and takes up space.

atom
The smallest part of an element that can exist alone. All matter is made up of atoms.

⊕ Name It!

energy
Light, electricity, and heat. Energy is used and produced in chemical reactions.

physics
The scientific study of both matter and energy in great detail.

states
All matter can exist in three different states: solid, liquid, or gas.

physical properties
Characteristics of matter, such as color, odor, taste, boiling point, and melting point.

chemical properties
The ways matter reacts with other types of matter in a chemical reaction.

States of Matter

All matter can exist in three different **states**: solid, liquid, or gas. Energy is required to change matter from one state to another. Let's think about water as an example. Water can be a liquid (for swimming or drinking), a solid (ice for ice skating or for snow cones), or a gas (clouds, fog, or steam). A lot of energy (heat) is needed to get water to boil and turn it into a gas called steam. We can heat up ice or snow, which will cause it to melt into liquid. Place some water in the freezer (that freezer uses electricity, which is energy) and the water will become solid ice. Did you figure out that the state of matter called *gas* doesn't mean the same as gas for the car? Car gas is actually a shortened form of the word *gasoline*, which is another type of chemical.

Properties of Matter

How can we tell one kind of matter apart from other kinds of matter? Sugar and salt look alike, but if you get them mixed up, a piece of candy wouldn't taste very good. There are some special characteristics that we can use to identify matter — and in a way, taste is one of them. These are called properties of matter by chemists. There are two types of properties of matter: physical properties and chemical properties.

Physical properties include characteristics like color, odor, taste, boiling point, and melting point. If we look at a piece of iron metal, we will usually see that it is solid. When the iron metal is solid, we say that it is in a solid state. It is very strong in this state and is used in making bridges, buildings, cars, and trucks. Solid iron melts at a very high temperature. This means that it has a melting point that is much higher than ice. However, when iron is heated enough, it does melt and become liquid iron, which can be formed into many useful objects and materials. Once iron cools back down below its melting point, it becomes solid again. This melting point is an example of a physical property. Although we can sense (see, smell, and taste) some properties, the most accurate and safest way for the

Lesson 3: Matter

chemist to examine physical properties is to use special equipment to measure them exactly.

Chemical properties, on the other hand, are the ways the matter reacts with other types of matter in a chemical reaction. Let's use iron again as an example. Iron reacts with oxygen, which makes rust. The part of iron that rusts is no longer iron. It's been changed into a new substance called ferric oxide. Some of the iron remains, but the rusty part has been chemically changed.

Review It

1. An easy way to recognize matter is that it has _____Weight_____ and takes up _____space_____.

2. Everything in this physical world can be placed in either of two categories: _____Matter_____ or _____energy_____.

3. All matter can exist in three different states: _____Solid_____, _____liquid_____, or _____gas_____.

4. There are some special characteristics that we can use to identify matter — and in a way, taste is one of them. These are called _____Properties_____ of matter by chemists.

5. _____Physical_____ properties include things like color, odor, taste, boiling point, and melting point.

Additional Notes

Hands-On:
Separating Compounds by Filtration

The grains of sand at the beach sometimes look like the grains of salt that we use for our food. However, everyone would agree that sand and salt certainly don't taste the same. That's because they are two entirely different chemical compounds. Let's say that on a trip to the beach for a picnic, you spilled the saltshaker into the sand. This is a problem since you really want some salt for your fried chicken picnic lunch. When you try to gather some of the salt back into the shaker, you get sand as well. The sand has contaminated the salt. This type of contamination problem occurs for chemists as well. Since chemists know the different physical properties of matter, they can figure out ways to separate things or remove the contamination. We can do that too.

Equipment Needed

- 2 teaspoons of salt (regular table salt)
- 1 teaspoon of fine sand
- bowl (like a cereal bowl)
- ordinary coffee filter
- funnel that will hold the filter in place
- clear 16-ounce glass jar or drinking glass
- aluminum pie pan
- 100 milliliters of water
- measuring cup

Lesson 3: Matter

Activity

Material	Taste Notes	Touch Notes	Other Notes
salt			
sand			

1. Spend a few minutes trying to separate some of the sand by the characteristics of taste and appearance.

2. Fill out characteristic chart.

3. Measure and add 100 milliliters of water to the sand and salt mixture and stir thoroughly for about one minute.

4. Place the coffee filter into the funnel.

5. Place the funnel in the glass jar.

6. Slowly pour the contents of the bowl into the filter-lined funnel.

7. Allow the liquid to pass through the filter into the glass jar. (Note: This takes a few minutes. It is not necessary to get all the liquid through.)

8. Take 1 teaspoon of the liquid that passed through the filter and put it onto the aluminum pie pan.

9. Allow the liquid in the pie pan to evaporate. This step may take a couple of days, but remember to come back and answer the following questions.

Additional Notes

Additional Notes

Think about It

1. Do you see the salt on the pie pan? Did you think the salt and sand could be separated?

   _____

   _____

2. Can you think of any other way that the sand and salt could be separated? How?

   _____

   _____

3. How do you think the salt was able to go through the filter?

   _____

   _____

4. Do you think all the salt was removed from the sand? Why or why not?

   _____

   _____

Lesson 3: Matter

Hands-On: (Easier Alternative)
Filtration Word Search

Sometimes the white sand on a beach sure looks like salt. Sand even looks like sugar. While on a picnic at the beach, somehow, you've spilled your salt and sugar into the sand. Your lunch wouldn't taste the same without salt for your chicken and sugar for your strawberries. You definitely don't want sand in your food. So, the only thing you can do is try to separate things the best you can. Try to find these words that are things that might be mixed up in the sand, along with your sugar and salt

```
A  C  F  S  T  I  C  K  S  R
S  A  N  D  D  R  I  S  H  O
S  T  O  I  S  U  G  A  R  P
S  B  A  R  T  F  I  S  H  E
E  U  G  R  S  H  E  L  L  S
A  N  G  E  F  D  B  U  B  L
W  C  R  A  B  I  K  D  U  F
E  S  R  O  G  R  S  K  G  I
E  D  C  R  C  T  T  H  S  L
D  C  H  E  M  K  S  A  L  T
```

SHELLS	SUGAR	ROCK	STARFISH
SAND	DIRT	BUGS	ROPE
CRAB	SEAWEED	FISH	SALT
STICKS			

✝ Scripture
Be imitators of God, therefore, as dearly loved children. (Ephesians 5:1)

◉ Discovery Zone
The temperature of water with ice cubes is exactly 32°F. If it is colder, the water will freeze. If it gets warmer, the ice will melt.

Lesson 4

Teaching Time:
Elementary Elements

Remember from the last lesson: everything is made of matter. Matter can be made entirely of the same kind of atoms. Matter can also be made of more than one kind of atom. When matter is made of one or more of the same kind of atoms, it is made of a single element. An **element** is the purest form of matter that exists. For example, nitrogen gas is made of one type of atom — the nitrogen atom.

> **Name It!**
> <u>element</u>
> *The purest form of matter that exists.*

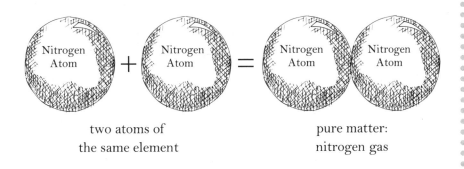

two atoms of the same element

pure matter: nitrogen gas

◆ **Name It!**
<u>compound</u>
A substance that is made up of two or more elements.

Another example of matter made of a single element is oxygen, which is made of one type of atom — oxygen.

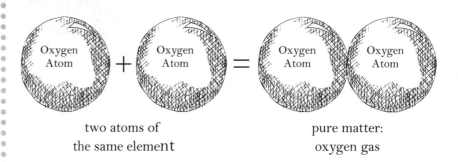

two atoms of the same element   pure matter: oxygen gas

When matter is made of more than one type of atom, it is called a compound. A compound is a substance, such as salt, that is made up of two or more elements. In the case of salt, the elements of chlorine and sodium combine to make the salt compound, called sodium chloride, which is what we use to salt our food.

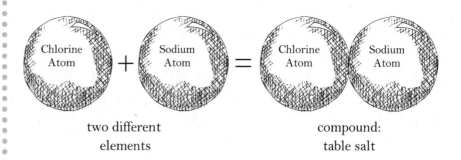

two different elements   compound: table salt

Another example of a compound is water, which is actually formed by the combining of two elements — hydrogen and oxygen.

Lesson 4: Elements

two different elements

compound: water

There are only 92 naturally occurring elements. There are also about 26 elements that have been made in the lab by changing parts of other elements. Even the ones that have been made in the lab are made from elements that already existed — just changed somewhat. As the elements were discovered, they were often named in a way that represents one of their properties. Element names are usually written in an abbreviated or shortened form by chemists, by using letters of the alphabet. This is called the symbol of the element. Some are easy to remember, such as O for oxygen, N for nitrogen, H for hydrogen, C for carbon, I for iodine, S for Sulfur, and Al for aluminum. Some symbols come from the Latin name for the element such as Au (aurum) for gold and Ag (argentum) for silver. All matter in the world and universe is made up of these elements. There is a list of the known elements, showing the chemical symbol and chemical name on pages 282 – 283.

Additional Notes

Review It

1. When matter is made of one or more of the same kind of atoms, it is made of a single _____.

2. When matter is made of more than one type of atom, it is called a _____.

Additional Notes

3. There are only _____ naturally occurring elements.

4. An element is the purest form of _____ that exists.

5. _____ made all of the naturally occurring elements.

Hands-On:
Making Element Cards

Keeping index cards is a good way to create study notes for any subject — especially chemistry. As we explore chemistry, we are going to make and use element cards. By recording information about elements on index cards, you can begin to expand your knowledge of chemistry and develop a database about each element. Beginning in lesson 1, we talked about several different elements. There are many more to learn about and much more to learn about each element. In this activity, we will make our starter set of cards of the elements we've discussed so far. You can add new element cards and new information as we go along in the lessons. You may also learn something about the elements from another book or source and write that information on your cards as well.

Equipment Needed

- 3x5 lined index cards

Lesson 4: Elements

Activity

1. Prepare element cards for each of the following elements — one card per element.
    - gold
    - silver
    - carbon
    - iron
    - oxygen
    - sodium
    - chlorine
    - nitrogen
    - iodine
    - sulfur
    - aluminum

2. On the front (unlined) side of the card, write the name of the element at the top. Using the periodic table in appendix A on page 284, write the correct symbol for that element in the center of the card in large letters. Toward the bottom of the card, write the labels for atomic number and atomic weight (which we will be studying later).

3. On the back of each card, write labels for characteristics/notes and interesting facts.

Your cards should look similar to this example:

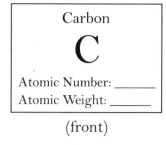
(front)

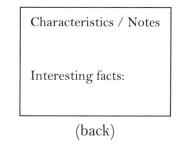
(back)

> **✝ Scripture**
> *For by him all things were created: things in heaven and on earth, visible and invisible...*
> *(Colossians 1:16a)*

> **◉ Discovery Zone**
> *The human body is made mostly of just four elements: hydrogen, oxygen, carbon, and nitrogen.*

Additional Notes

Reminder: Keep your cards handy during the lessons and update them when you learn new information about an element or make a new card when a new element is mentioned in a lesson.

Lesson 5
MIXTURES AND COMPOUNDS

Teaching Time:
Don't Get Mixed with Mixtures and Compounds

Remember, all matter is made out of elements. Sometimes matter is made entirely of atoms of the same element. Sometimes matter is made of atoms from two or more elements. When matter is made of more than one element, it must be one of two things: a compound or a mixture. The differences are pretty easy to see, if you know what to look for.

Compounds

A compound is made up of two or more elements. These elements are chemically combined together to form a new substance. To be chemically combined means that a bond or connection exists between the elements, which keeps them together under normal cir-

> **⊕ Name It!**
> **mixtures**
> *Made of two or more pure substances or compounds that are physically combined (mixed) together but not chemically bonded.*

cumstances. There are millions of different compounds. We saw two examples in the previous lesson. One was salt, which is called sodium chloride in chemistry terms. It is made by combining the atoms of the element sodium with atoms of the element chlorine, and it is held together by a chemical bond.

Mixtures

When two or more pure compounds physically combine together (like sand and salt), we have a mixture. **Mixtures** are made of two or more pure substances or compounds that are physically combined (mixed) together but not chemically bonded. Remember in the previous lesson that we got sand mixed up with our salt on a trip to the beach. Sand is actually a pure compound called silicon dioxide that is made of the atoms of the element silicon bonded to atoms of the element oxygen.

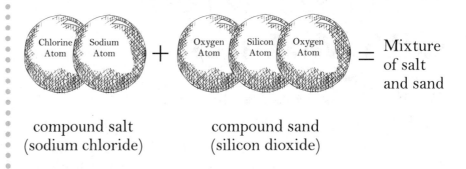

compound salt (sodium chloride)   compound sand (silicon dioxide)

Although it might take some time, we know from our Hands-On in lesson 3 that we can separate the sand from the salt and once again have the two pure compounds of salt (sodium chloride) and sand (silicon dioxide).

Mixtures aren't just for solids and liquids. They can also occur in gases. The air we breathe is made up of many different gases, each a pure compound on its own. Air is composed of mostly nitrogen, but it also has oxygen (that we need for our bodies), carbon dioxide (a compound containing carbon and oxygen that the plants use), and a few other gases. Here is some

Lesson 5: Mixtures and Compounds

interesting news: mixtures can even be composed of a gas, solids, and a liquid. Can you think of an example? How about a soft drink? It is the mixture of carbon dioxide (gas) with water (liquid) and sugar (solid) and other secret ingredients (other compounds) for flavoring of course. Here are seven types of mixtures:

- Liquid mixed with liquid
- Solid mixed with solid
- Gas mixed with gas
- Liquid mixed with gas
- Liquid mixed with solid
- Gas mixed with solid
- Gas mixed with solid and liquid

Review It

1. When matter is made of more than one element, it must be one of two things: a _____ or a _____.

2. When two or more pure compounds physically combine together (like sand and salt), we have a _____.

3. A _____ is made up of two or more elements. These elements are chemically combined together to form a new substance.

Additional Notes

Additional Notes

4. Salt (called sodium chloride) is made from the combining of atoms of the element _____ with atoms of the element _____ and held together by a chemical bond.

5. Mixtures can even be between a _____, a _____, and a _____.

Hands-On:
Examining Mixtures and Compounds

We find things combined together all the time. A chemist also finds things combined. It is important to be able to recognize when something is combined to form a chemical compound and when it is simply a mixture.

Equipment Needed

- 2 teaspoons of cooking oil
- 1 teaspoon of sugar
- 1 teaspoon of fine sand
- 1 teaspoon of salt
- 1 teaspoon of mustard
- water
- six small bowls (like cereal bowls)
- paper adhesive labels

Lesson 5: Mixtures and Compounds

Activity

Sample	Compound/Mixture	Mixture Type	Notes
sugar	compound		
mustard	mixture		
salt	compound		
air in the room	mixture		
water	compound		
cooking oil and water combined	mixture		
sand and salt combined	mixture		

1. In a bowl, place about 1 teaspoon of mustard and label "Mustard Mixture."

2. In a second bowl, combine 1 teaspoon of sand with one teaspoon of salt and label "Sand/Salt Mixture."

3. In a third bowl, place about 1 teaspoon of sugar and label "Sugar Compound."

4. In fourth bowl, place about 1 teaspoon of salt and label "Salt Compound."

5. In a fifth bowl, add some water and label "Water Compound."

6. In a sixth bowl, combine 2 teaspoons of cooking oil with 2 teaspoons of water and label "Water/Oil Mixture."

Additional Notes

Additional Notes

7. Take a few minutes to examine each of the bowls and think about what is inside.

8. Complete the chart on the previous page with your notes and observations.

9. For the mixtures, indicate what type of mixture you think it is (for example: solid-solid, solid-liquid, liquid-liquid, gas-gas, gas-liquid, etc). This doesn't apply to compounds.

10. Write a short note about your choice of the type of mixture.

Think about It

1. What type of mixture did you indicate for mustard? It appears to be a liquid, but if you examine the label on the mustard jar in the refrigerator, you may find that it is composed of more than one liquid, as well as more than one type of solid.

   _____

   _____

2. Normally air is thought of as a mixture of various gases. However, sometimes there may be dust or smoke in the air. Dust and smoke are made of very small solids. So, what type of mixture is it?

   _____

   _____

Lesson 5: Mixtures and Compounds

3. Did you notice that the water and the cooking oil mixture separated into a water layer and an oil layer? Were you surprised?

_____

_____

✝ Scripture
For God so loved the world that he gave his one and only Son, that whoever believes in him shall not perish but have eternal life. (John 3:16)

◉ Discovery Zone
The elements of phosphorus and calcium together make up 75% of the human body's mineral content.

Unit One Wrap-Up
Show What You Know!

1. Chemistry is the structured and formal study of _____.
    a. medicine
    b. matter
    c. baseball

2. A _____ is a specially trained scientist that studies and works with matter.
    a. chemist
    b. veterinarian
    c. biologist

3. Organic chemistry is the study of matter that contains a substance called _____.
    a. dog food
    b. carbon
    c. oxygen

4. When chemists study the matter of living things, it is called _____.
    a. gardening
    b. physical chemistry
    c. biochemistry

Study Notes

Study Notes

5. A _____ is a piece of scientific glassware that is shaped similar to a drinking glass, holds liquids, can be heated, provides some measuring, and has a spout for pouring.
    a. beaker
    b. salt shaker
    c. flask

6. Various pieces of glassware can be connected together allowing the flow of liquids and gases from one container to another by using a _____.
    a. garden hose
    b. glass tubing
    c. pipette

7. A _____ allows the easy collection of liquids poured from a container and then passes some portion of the liquid through to a container with a smaller top opening.
    a. pie pan
    b. beaker
    c. funnel

8. Chemists use a long cylinder with measurements marked on its side to measure liquid. It is called a _____.
    a. graduated cylinder
    b. tin can
    c. Erlenmeyer flask

9. An easy way to recognize matter is that it has _____ and takes up space.
    a. a number
    b. money
    c. weight

Unit One Wrap-Up

10. Everything in this physical world is either energy or
 _____.
    a. lazy
    b. atoms
    c. matter

11. All matter can exist in three different states:
 _____, _____, or
 _____.
    a. animal, mineral, vegetable
    b. solid, liquid, gas
    c. proton, neutron, electron

12. There are some special characteristics that we can use to identify matter — and in a way, taste is one of them. These are called _____ of matter by chemists.
    a. behaviors
    b. properties
    c. mysteries

13. When matter is made of one or more of the same kind of atoms, it is made of a single _____.
    a. proton
    b. element
    c. color

14. When matter is made of more than one type of atom, it is called a _____.
    a. goofy matter
    b. compound
    c. molecule

Study Notes

Study Notes

15. There are only _____ naturally occurring elements.
    a. 144
    b. 92
    c. 5

16. An element is the purest form of _____ that exists.
    a. ice cream
    b. energy
    c. matter

17. _____ made all of the naturally occurring elements.
    a. Chemists
    b. God
    c. The army

18. When matter is made of more than one element, it must be one of two things: _____ or _____.
    a. a big mistake, an accident
    b. a molecule, an atom
    c. a mixture, a compound

19. When two or more pure compounds physically combine together (like sand and salt), we have a _____.
    a. problem
    b. compound
    c. mixture

Unit One Wrap-Up

20. A _____ is made up of two or more elements. These elements are chemically combined together to form a new substance.
    a. compound
    b. liquid
    c. mixture

Study Notes

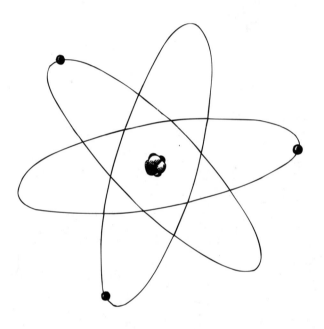

Unit Two
Atoms and Molecules

Now that we have a pretty good understanding of what chemistry and matter are, we can begin exploring the pieces and parts that make chemistry interesting. We can certainly see and touch the matter that makes up the universe, but in this unit we will find out just what's inside the matter. The stuff that you can't see is what is doing all the work in chemistry — the atoms. These atoms connect with other atoms to make molecules. The molecules are what make up medicine, food, clothing, living things, rocks, minerals, water, and even the air we breathe. These tiny building blocks are held together in a miraculous way. Scientists can describe the atoms and the molecules, but it is God who created them.

Additional Notes

Upon completing unit 2, the student should understand:

- The composition of atoms
- Atomic number and atomic weight
- How to use the periodic table
- The structure and form of molecules

Unit 2 Vocabulary Words

- nucleus
- extranuclear region
- proton
- neutron
- electron
- atomic number
- ions
- atomic mass number
- isotope
- periodic table of the elements
- periodic law of chemistry

Materials Needed for This Unit

- ten Styrofoam balls — approximately 2 inches in diameter
- four Styrofoam balls — approximately 1 inch in diameter
- several toothpicks
- three plastic drinking straws
- colored markers or tempera (water-based) paint
- pack of 3x5 index cards
- pencil
- recipe and ingredients for making sugar cookies or butter cookies
- several packages of M&M's

Lesson 6

Teaching Time:
The Amazing Atom

One atom is the smallest piece of an element we can have. This is actually a pretty good definition of an atom. The smallest size or piece of gold we can have is one atom of gold. The smallest piece of iron we can have is one atom of iron. We cannot have a smaller piece of iron than one atom of iron.

Regions of the Atom

Think about the atom as being made up of two distinct regions. The first region we will call the **nucleus**, which means the center. The second region is called the **extranuclear region**, which is the area outside the nucleus, but still part of the atom. Inside the nucleus of the atom, there are two types of particles. One type of particle is called a **neutron,** and the other type of particle is called a **proton**. Protons and neutrons are the subatomic particles that give weight to an atom. Outside of the nucleus, in the extranuclear region, there is only one type of particle, which

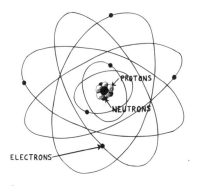

➜ **Name It!**

<u>nucleus</u>
The center of the atom.

<u>extranuclear region</u>
The area outside the nucleus, but still part of the atom.

<u>neutron</u>
A type of particle found in the nucleus of an atom; it has a neutral electrical charge.

> **Name It!**
>
> **proton**
> *A type of particle found in the nucleus of an atom; it has a positive electrical charge.*
>
> **electron**
> *The only type of particle found in the extranuclear region of an atom; it has a negative electrical charge.*

is called an **electron**. All three types of particles (called subatomic particles since they are parts of the atom) are very important because they give each atom its identity and its nature (sort of like its appearance and personality). Let's take a closer look at these subatomic particles.

Protons

Protons were the first of the subatomic particles to be discovered in 1886 by a German physicist named Eugene Goldstein. It is always important to remember that even though protons weren't discovered until 1886, they already existed as a creation of God. They have been doing their jobs in the atoms and in matter since the earth was created. The discovery of protons is another way for us to see the beauty and complexity of God's universe.

Neutrons

Neutrons were discovered in 1932 by the English physicist James Chadwick. A neutron has the same weight as a proton and is the other contributor to the weight of the atom. These two particles are found together inside the nucleus of an atom. There can be many protons and neutrons in a single atom. For example, the element carbon has 6 protons and 6 neutrons. The element mercury has 80 protons and 120 neutrons.

Electrons

Electrons move very fast around the nucleus in a region we can call the extranuclear region, which is the space outside of the nucleus. The electrons actually travel near the speed of light. The most energetic electrons are farther away from the nucleus than the less energetic ones. So, the lower energy electrons are usually close to the nucleus in what is called an inner shell. The higher energy electrons are found in additional shells as we go farther from the nucleus into the outer part of the extranuclear

Lesson 6: Atoms

region. Atoms with many electrons have up to seven shells for all their electrons to have space to move about.

Another important feature of the atom is its electrical charge. A positive (+) or negative (-) charge on an atom makes it able to join other atoms that are positively or negatively charged to make a compound, such as table salt. Within the nucleus, the protons carry a positive charge. So for every proton there is one positive (+). To keep the atom itself uncharged, there must be something to counteract that positive. Neutrons are neutral and have no charge (0), so they can't help balance the proton's positive charge. That's why those particles are called neutrons. So the only particles left are the electrons. The charge on each electron is one negative (-). As long as the number of electrons and protons are the same, they cancel one another out and the entire atom is neutral and carries no charge. The number of electrons is equal to the number of protons when the atom is in its uncharged state.

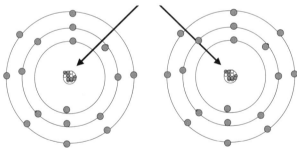

Uncharged chlorine atom (Cl) with 17 negatively charged electrons and 17 positively charged protons.

Negatively charged chlorine atom (Cl-) with 18 negatively charged electrons and 17 positively charged protons.

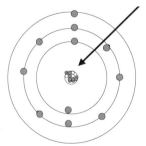 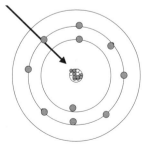

Uncharged sodium atom (Na) with 11 negatively charged electrons and 11 positively charged protons.

Positively charged sodium atom (Na+) with only 10 negatively charged electrons and 11 positively charged protons.

Additional Notes

Additional Notes

Review It

1. The _____ is the smallest piece of an element you can have.

2. The region in the center of the atom is the _____. The outer region of the atom is called the _____.

3. Inside the nuclear region of the atom, there are two types of particles. One type of particle is called _____ and the other type of particle is called _____.

4. Within the nucleus, the protons carry a _____ charge. Neutrons are neutral and have no charge (0), and electrons have a _____ charge.

5. The number of electrons is _____ to the number of protons, when the atom is in its uncharged state.

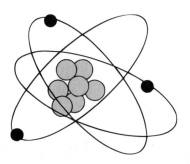

Lesson 6: Atoms

Hands-On:
Building Atomic Models

Models are ways to represent things and can help us to get a better idea of how things look. Maybe you have made some models before, such as model cars, birds, or airplanes. Models are usually not the same size as the actual car or airplane, but they show what they look like. Scientists also make models to represent things. It helps them to see and understand things better. We are going to make some models of atoms. Instead of the models being smaller than the real thing (like a model car), these models will be a lot larger.

A very easy atom model to make is lithium. Lithium is a fairly small and simple atom since it has three protons, four neutrons, and three electrons. Here is a diagram of a lithium atom to give you an idea of how it is arranged. The protons and neutrons are in the nucleus (the center of the figure), and the electrons occupy the space outside the nucleus. The elliptical lines represent the movement of the electrons around the nucleus. However, the electrons actually don't travel in an exact orbit.

Equipment Needed

- seven Styrofoam balls — approximately 2 inches in diameter (available at craft stores)
- three Styrofoam balls — approximately 1 inch in diameter
- several toothpicks
- three plastic drinking straws
- colored markers or tempera (water-based) paint

Additional Notes

✝ Scripture
And the words of the Lord are flawless, like silver refined in a furnace of clay, purified seven times. (Psalm 12:6).

◉ Discovery Zone
Did you ever wonder why the element gold is such an expensive treasure? It is because it is so hard to find. It may take 20,000 pounds of rock to get just one ounce of gold.

Activity

1. Paint or color three of the 2-inch balls blue. These will be protons.

2. Paint or color the four other 2-inch balls yellow. These will be the neutrons.

3. Paint or color the 1-inch balls red. These will be the electrons.

4. Using the toothpicks, connect the protons (blue balls) with the neutrons (yellow balls) so they are touching each other. There should be no gap between the balls.

5. Insert one end of the plastic drinking straw into each of the electrons (red balls).

6. Insert the other end of the plastic drinking straw into a proton. Add a little glue if necessary to hold them in place.

Think about It

1. How does the model help you understand the way atoms look?

   _____

   _____

2. What things about the models aren't correctly representing atoms? For example, do you think the particles have color? What about the size of the balls? Anything else?

   _____

Lesson 6: Atoms

_____

3. What things about the model do you think are good representations of the atom?

_____

_____

4. What would you need in order to make a model of a lead atom, which has 82 protons and 125 neutrons?

_____

_____

Lesson 7
ATOMIC NUMBER

Teaching Time:
Can You Count on the Atomic Number?

Each of the elements has a number assigned to it called an atomic number. Each element has a unique atomic number. This number gives us two important pieces of information about the element. The **atomic number** is equal to the number of protons in one atom of the element. For example, the element of carbon has an atomic number of 6. This means that in an atom of carbon there are six protons. The element nitrogen has an atomic number of 7. Therefore, an atom of nitrogen contains seven protons. If somehow the nitrogen lost a proton, it would only have six protons. If it only has six protons, then it is no longer nitrogen. So, what is it? It is carbon. See, the number of protons (the atomic number) is what makes an element unique. Isn't that amazing how only one proton can change the element? The second important piece of information that we get from the atomic number is the

➔ Name It!
<u>atomic number</u>
Each element has an atomic number. It is equal to the number of protons in one atom of the element.

63

> **Name It!**
> <u>ions</u>
> *Atoms with extra electrons or those missing electrons.*

number of electrons. Remember, the number of protons in an atom equals the number of electrons.

Isn't God truly all knowing and awesome to think of something so beautiful and logical as the atom? There is beauty in each of the 92 naturally occurring elements and the way in which God created them, each with special properties and for a special purpose.

Electrical Charge and Balance

Remember from lesson 6, the number of electrons is equal to the number of protons, which means the electrical charge is balanced. If we know the atomic number of an element, we also know the number of electrons. Sodium has an atomic number of 11. It has 11 protons and 11 electrons. Remember that electrons have a negative (−) charge and protons have a positive (+) charge. Chlorine has 17 protons that provide a total positive (+) charge of 17. Chlorine also has 17 electrons and a total negative (−) charge of 17. The positive protons are cancelled by the negative electrons and the total charge of the chlorine atom equals no charge (0), which makes it a neutral atom.

Sometimes atoms lose electrons. When that happens, they have a positive (+) charge, since they now have more protons than electrons. Sometimes an atom gets an extra electron and that makes the atom negatively (−) charged. Atoms in this condition (missing electrons or having extra electrons) are called **ions** (pronounced EYE-ons).

Review It

1. Each of the elements has a number assigned to it called an

   _____.

Lesson 7: Atomic Number

2. The atomic number is equal to the number of _____ in one atom of the element.

3. The number of protons is what makes an element _____.

4. If somehow a nitrogen atom lost a proton, it would only have six protons. If it only had six protons, then it would be _____.

5. Atoms that are missing electrons or have extra electrons are called _____.

Additional Notes

Hands-On:
Labeling the Subatomic Particles

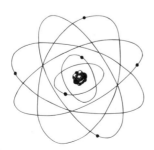

Additional Notes

Carbon's atomic number is 6. It has six protons, six neutrons, and six electrons.

Equipment Needed

- paper
- pencil

Activity

1. See the drawing of the carbon atom at the start of this section. Draw it and label the atom using the following terms: nuclear region, extranuclear region, proton and neutron (you can't tell them apart), and electron.

2. Nitrogen is atomic number 7. It has seven protons, seven neutrons, and seven electrons. Draw a nitrogen atom and label all the parts.

Think about It

1. Is there anything about the nitrogen atom that is different from the carbon atom?

   _____

   _____

2. Do you think the electrons go around in orbit or generally bounce around in a particular area?

   _____

Lesson 7: Atomic Number

Hands-On: (A Fun Alternative)
Atomic Cookies

Making models is a great way to help understand how things look. There are many ways to make models of atoms — some even taste good. In this Hands-On, you can make giant atoms — and then eat them! By using different colored M&M's, these cookies can become edible models of the carbon and nitrogen atoms.

Equipment Needed

- recipe and ingredients for making cookies
- several packages of colored M&M's

Activity

1. Prepare cookie dough for you favorite cookie.

2. Roll the dough out and shape the cookies into round shapes about 4 inches in diameter.

3. For the carbon atoms, place six red M&M's (protons) and six blue M&M's (neutrons) close together in the center of the round cookie dough. This is the nucleus. Around the edge, place six brown M&M's (the electrons).

4. Do the same thing for the nitrogen atoms, but use seven protons, seven neutrons, and seven electrons.

5. Bake according to the recipe directions.

As you eat the cookies, discuss that they are models of atoms. Think about the protons, neutrons, and electrons. Try to identify each cookie correctly as a carbon or nitrogen atom.

✝ Scripture
Choose my instruction instead of silver, knowledge rather than choice gold. (Proverbs 8:10)

◉ Discovery Zone
In the early 1960s there were two very funny, G-rated movies made about chemistry that you might want to see. One is The Absent Minded Professor *starring Fred MacMurray. The other is* The Nutty Professor *starring Jerry Lewis. These were both remade in the 1990s, but the originals are definitely the best ones to see.*

Lesson 8
ATOMIC MASS

Teaching Time:
A Massive Mass

In the last lesson we learned about the importance of an element's atomic number. The atomic number is equal to the number of protons in one atom of the element. Carbon has an atomic number of 6, therefore we know that an atom of carbon has six protons. Besides the atomic number, every element also has an **atomic mass number**. This is equal to the number of protons plus the number of neutrons.

Scientists have figured out the mass number for all the elements and we can easily look up that number in a table. Carbon has a mass number of 12. Since we know that carbon has an atomic number of 6 (since it has six protons), we can subtract the six protons from the atomic mass number to find the number of neutrons, which is six in a carbon atom. The formula is:

→ Name It!
<u>atomic mass number</u>
The number of protons plus the number of neutrons added together.

atomic mass number = number of
protons + number of neutrons

69

◆ **Name It!**
<u>isotope</u>
An atom that has gained neutrons.

This is an important way to determine the number of neutrons in an element. Sometimes the number of neutrons is the same as the number of protons (for example, carbon, oxygen, helium), but the number of neutrons isn't *always* the same as the number of protons.

One other thing to know about the atom is its atomic weight. It's a little complicated to understand, but the weight of an atom only comes from the protons and neutrons. The electrons have almost no weight, so they don't contribute to the weight of the atom. Sometimes the elements can temporarily gain a couple of neutrons. This doesn't change the element into something else, but it does change its weight. When an element gains neutrons, it is called an **isotope**, but it remains the same element with the same atomic number. People are a lot like isotopes. We can gain a little weight, but we are still the same people. Because the elements can occur as isotopes, the exact weight can vary. Therefore, an element's atomic weight is given in charts as an average weight. However, by simply rounding to the nearest whole number, we can always get back to the atomic mass number. Here are some examples in a chart that puts it all together:

Element	Atomic Number	Atomic Mass Number	Atomic Weight	Number of Protons	Number of Neutrons	Number of Electrons
carbon	6	12	12.01	6	6	6
hydrogen	1	1	1.01	1	0	1
oxygen	8	16	16.00	8	8	8
nitrogen	7	14	14.01	7	7	7
uranium	92	238	238.03	92	146	92
lead	82	207	207.2	82	125	82

Lesson 8: Atomic Mass

Using various scientific instruments, scientists have determined the atomic mass of every element. This information is presented in various tables including a very important one called the periodic table of the elements, which we will look at in the next lesson.

Review It

1. Electrons have almost no _____.

2. The mass number of the atom comes almost entirely from the mass of the _____ and the mass of the _____.

3. The _____ _____ _____ for any element is equal to the number of protons plus the number of neutrons in a single atom of the element.

4. Using various _____ _____, scientists have determined the atomic mass of every element.

5. Information about the atomic mass and atomic number of elements is presented in a table called the _____ _____ of the _____.

Additional Notes

Additional Notes

Hands-On:
Catch Up on Element Cards

In lesson 4 we started our element card collection. These cards can be very useful in the future, even when you are a college student. Scientists themselves often use notecards for indexing and making notes about their research. Of course, the computer now helps a lot with some of the note taking.

Equipment Needed

- pack of 3x5 index cards
- pencil

Activity

1. Go through the previous lessons and make a card for every element we have mentioned (except for the complete list of elements and abbreviations from lesson 4, of course). You should have quite a few.

2. Complete as much information as you can for each element. For some this may only be the element name and symbol.

3. Review the cards and think about what you know about each element.

Lesson 8: Atomic Mass

4. Keep the cards in a card box or bound with a rubber band and remember to update them as we continue our study of chemistry.

Think about It

1. Are you surprised at the number of elements that you have learned something about?

   _____

   _____

2. Does any part of an atom interest you more than another?

   _____

   _____

✝ Scripture
Great is the Lord and most worthy of praise; his greatness no one can fathom. (Psalm 145:3)

◉ Discovery Zone
Scientists that study the electrons, protons, and neutrons are called particle physicists.

Lesson 9

PERIODIC TABLE

Teaching Time:
A Peek at the Periodic Table

We have learned that each element has some important characteristics. These are:

- atomic weight,
- atomic mass number (equaling protons plus neutrons),
- atomic number (equaling the number of protons),
- chemical symbol (one- or two-letter abbreviation), and
- chemical and physical properties.

By the late 1800s, many elements and their properties, such as atomic mass, were known. Chemists wanted to arrange these elements in an orderly and meaningful way in a table, which was accomplished in 1869. In the early 1900s, some studies helped scientists better understand the importance of an element's atomic number. Today the **periodic table of the elements**

◆ Name It!
<u>periodic table of the elements</u>
Sometimes called the periodic chart; this table is a list of elements arranged according to the element's atomic number.

> **⊕ Name it!**
> **periodic law of chemistry**
> *States that when the elements are arranged in a table according to their atomic number, elements with similar properties occur at regular intervals called periods.*

The periodic table is located in appendix A on page 284.

(sometimes called the periodic chart or periodic table) is arranged according to the element's atomic number (atomic number 1 is first, atomic number 2 is second, and so forth). The periodic table contains characteristics for each element — atomic weight, atomic number, and chemical symbol. The table is a chart with boxes. Each box represents an element. Inside each box there is the symbol of the element; the atomic number, located above the symbol; and the atomic mass, located below the symbol.

In addition to being arranged in the order of their atomic number, the elements are also arranged in a way that represents their properties. This is why the periodic table isn't just a rectangular table; it is oddly shaped. We can think of the periodic table as being laid out in an organized way, similar to the way many grocery stores group foods in certain areas to make it easy to shop. For example, the fresh fruits and vegetables are usually located on the far right side of the store. The frozen foods and dairy products are usually located on the far left side of the store, so you can put them in your cart after you have just about completed shopping. In the center of the store there are many other food aisles, all grouped together by their similar properties. Cereals and breakfast foods are in an aisle together; juices, coffees, and teas are in an aisle together; cookies, candy, crackers, and snacks are together. Get the idea? The grocery store is arranged in a sort of periodic table of foods.

Periods

The periodic table actually represents the **periodic law of chemistry**, which states that when the elements are arranged in a table according to their atomic number, elements with similar properties occur at regular intervals called periods. The periodic table has seven horizontal rows of elements, called periods, that are numbered 1 – 7. Remember, in lesson 6 we explained that an atom could have as many as seven shells where the electrons move around. The row or period number tells us how many shells an element has for its electrons. The elements in period one all have one shell. Elements in period two all have two shells and so on. Since there are only seven periods in the periodic table, can you figure the greatest possible number of shells there can be for any element? If you think there are only seven shells possible, you are correct. The reason for these periods is that the number of electrons in the outer shell of atoms follows a pattern. Some elements have their outer shell full, so they are grouped together. Some atoms have only one electron in their outer shell, and they are grouped together. The number of electrons in the outer shell represents how reactive an element is. In other words, how *interested* is that element in getting together with another element?

Groups

The elements are also arranged into groups. Roman numerals and letters are used to label the groups. Like the grocery store, the elements are arranged in the groups (like aisles) by their similarities. Metals are on the left side of the periodic table and non-metals on the right side. Much of the nature of an element is reflected in its position in the periodic table. For example, if we look at the first group (Group IA), represented on the far left side of the table, we can see a family of metals beginning with lithium (Li), then sodium (Na), and so on. We know that in Group IA, the more reactive elements are lower in the column and the less reactive ones are higher. If we look at the far right side of the table we see another family called the noble gases of helium, neon, argon, krypton, xenon, and radon. Noble gases don't usually form chemical compounds. There are many important and interesting things to learn about the periodic table, but most of that is on a college level of chemistry. However, we can still learn a little about how the table looks and what it represents.

You might notice that there are two series of elements that are listed below the rest of the elements in the periodic table.

Additional Notes

Additional Notes

This is the way they are usually represented to save space in presenting the chart.

Review It

1. The periodic table of the elements is arranged according to the _____.

2. Each box in the periodic table contains atomic _____, atomic _____, and chemical _____, for each element.

3. Arrangement of the elements in the periodic table actually represents the _____ _____ of chemistry.

4. The far right side contains a family called the _____ gases.

5. The first period represented on the far left side of the table is a family of _____.

Lesson 9: Periodic Table

Hands-On: Using the Periodic Table

Besides being a chart that contains information about each element, the periodic table depicts the general natures of the elements. The elements are actually arranged in a way that can show us how reactive they are. Using the information contained in the lesson material and the periodic table in appendix A, we can make some predictions about various elements.

Equipment Needed

- pencil

Activity

1. The chart on the next page lists some elements. Find each one in the periodic table in appendix A.

2. Complete the chart.

3. Indicate whether the element is a metal or a non-metal.

4. Indicate the specific location in the periodic table (for example, aluminum is in Period 3 and Group IIIA).

(Note: You might also want to refer to the list of elements and their symbols in appendix A on pages 282 – 283.)

Additional Notes

The periodic table is located in appendix A on page 284.

Element	Metal or Non-Metal	Specific Location in the Periodic Table
sodium (Na)		
francium (Fr)		
chlorine (Cl)		
iodine (I)		
lead (Pb)		
copper (Cu)		
nitrogen (N)		
krypton (Kr)		
uranium (U)		
boron (B)		

Think about It

1. Do you find the periodic table easy to use?

   _____

   _____

Lesson 19: Solids and Liquids

2. What things about the periodic table are easy to understand?

   _____

   _____

3. What things about the periodic table are hard to understand?

   _____

   _____

✝ Scripture
The heavens declare the glory of God; the skies proclaim the work of his hands. (Psalm 19:1)

◉ Discovery Zone
Most of the elements are actually metals. The metals outnumber the non-metals about four to one.

Lesson 10

MOLECULES

Teaching Time:
The Marvelous Molecule

In the previous lessons, we have already seen some examples of molecules. Remember the two atoms of oxygen that make O_2? How about two hydrogen atoms coming together with an oxygen atom to form water (H_2O)? We know that atoms of the same element can come together and atoms of different elements can come together. In either case, what is formed is called a molecule. A **molecule** is defined as two or more atoms joined together.

The word *molecule* is also a measure of the amount of substance you have. Using our example of water, the two atoms of hydrogen are joined with one atom of oxygen to make exactly one molecule of water. The reason two hydrogen atoms join with only one oxygen atom is because of the location of the electrons on the hydrogen atom and oxygen atom. The location of the electrons is important in establishing a bond (the way

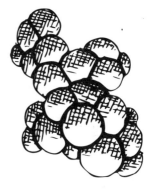

➲ **Name It!**
<u>molecule</u>
Two or more atoms joined together.

83

Additional Notes

atoms are joined). Oxygen has two electrons that are in position to hold on to another atom. So, it holds on to two hydrogen atoms. We will explain all about this in the next lesson.

H_2O and O_2 are examples of small molecules. But some molecules can be quite large. Glucose, which is a type of sugar, is a pretty large molecule — $C_6H_{12}O_6$. We see from this formula that there are 6 carbon atoms, 12 hydrogen atoms, and 6 oxygen atoms in one glucose molecule. Some molecules are made of thousands of atoms, such as the molecule hemoglobin, which is found in blood. We will explore many kinds of molecules in our other lessons.

Review It

1. _____ is defined as two or more atoms joined together.

2. The word *molecule* is also a measure of the amount of _____ you have.

3. H_2O and O_2 are examples of _____ molecules.

4. Two atoms of hydrogen joined with one atom of oxygen makes exactly one molecule of _____.

5. We know that atoms of the same _____ can come together and atoms of different _____ can come together to form molecules.

Lesson 10: Molecules

Hands-On:
Building Molecular Models

When we made a model of an atom in lesson 6, we were able to see the arrangement of the atomic particles a little better. We can do the same thing by making a model of a molecule. Be careful not to get mixed up between atoms and molecules. Remember, a molecule is made of more than one atom. To make a model of a molecule, we will forget about the neutrons, protons, and electrons. One way scientists make models of molecules is by designating a single ball as one atom. Inside the ball, you will have to imagine the neutrons, protons, and electrons — but, we won't be seeing them. So, for the molecular model, the balls will be atoms and the connection between the balls will represent the bonds between atoms.

Equipment Needed

- three Styrofoam balls — approximately 2 inches in diameter
- two Styrofoam balls — approximately 1 inch in diameter
- a few toothpicks
- colored markers

Activity
Build an Oxygen (O_2) Molecule Model

1. Print the letter "O" on two of the 2-inch balls. These will represent oxygen atoms.

Additional Notes

Additional Notes

2. Connect the two oxygen atoms together with a toothpick so that the two balls touch.

Your oxygen model will look something like this:

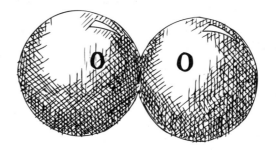

Build a Water (H_2O) Molecule Model

1. Print the letter "O" on the remaining 2-inch ball. This will represent the oxygen atom.

2. Print the letter "H" on the two 1-inch balls. These will represent hydrogen atoms.

3. Using toothpicks, connect one hydrogen atom to one side of the oxygen atom, and connect the other hydrogen atom to the other side of the oxygen atom. Be sure the hydrogen atoms are touching the oxygen.

Your water molecule will look something like this:

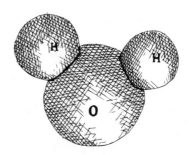

Lesson 10: Molecules

Think about It

1. Why do you think the balls representing the oxygen atoms are bigger than the ones representing the hydrogen atoms?

   _____

   _____

2. When you take a drink of water or take a shower, will you think about the millions of H_2O molecules?

   _____

   _____

3. Explain what is inside of each of the balls that represent the atoms?

   _____

   _____

4. How many protons, neutrons, and electrons are there in each of the balls that represent the two kinds of atoms?

   _____

   _____

✝ **Scripture**
The sea is his, for he made it, and his hands formed the dry land. (Psalm 95:5)

◉ **Discovery Zone**
Astronauts fly into space on special missions to collect information and study the stars and planets. How many astronauts do you think are chemists? You might be surprised. You can use the Internet and do a search on the words astronaut chemist *to find out more.*

Unit Two Wrap-Up
Show What You Know!

1. The _____ is the smallest piece of an element you can have.
    a. atom
    b. molecule
    c. bread crumb

2. The region in the center of the atom is the _____.
    a. core
    b. infield
    c. nuclear region

3. The outer region of the atom is called the _____.
    a. extranuclear region
    b. scary place
    c. molecule

4. Inside the nucleus of the atom, there are two types of particles. One type of particle is called _____ and the other type of particle is called _____.
    a. dust, dirt
    b. neutron, proton
    c. proton, electron

Study Notes

Study Notes

5. The protons carry a _____ charge.
   a. negative
   b. battery
   c. positive

6. The number of electrons is _____ the number of protons when the atom is in its uncharged state.
   a. equal to
   b. greater than
   c. trying to count

7. Each of the elements has a number assigned to it called an _____.
   a. atomic clock
   b. atomic fireball
   c. atomic number

8. The atomic number is equal to the number of _____ in one atom of the element.
   a. protons
   b. neutrons
   c. jelly beans

9. The number of protons (the atomic number) is what makes an element _____.
   a. unique
   b. expensive
   c. atomic

10. Atoms that are missing electrons or have extra electrons are called _____.
    a. messed up
    b. ions
    c. protons

Unit Two Wrap-Up

11. Electrons have almost no _____.
    a. charge
    b. money
    c. weight

12. The mass number of the atom comes almost entirely from the mass of the _____ and the mass of the _____.
    a. shell zone, electrons
    b. beans, hotdogs
    c. protons, neutrons

13. Using various _____, scientists have determined the atomic mass of every element.
    a. scientific instruments
    b. good guesses
    c. dangerous experiments

14. Information about the atomic mass and atomic number of elements is presented in a table called the _____.
    a. scientist's dictionary
    b. crossword puzzle
    c. periodic table

15. The periodic table of the elements is arranged according to the elements' _____.
    a. birth date
    b. atomic weight
    c. atomic number

Study Notes

Study Notes

16. Each box in the periodic table contains atomic _____, atomic _____, and chemical _____ for each element.
    a. weight, number, symbol
    b. fireball, energy, symbol
    c. energy, weight, symbol

17. The far right side of the periodic table contains a family called the _____ gases.
    a. important
    b. explosive
    c. noble

18. A _____ is defined as two or more atoms joined together.
    a. molecule
    b. chocolate chip cookie
    c. proton

19. H_2O and O_2 are examples of _____ molecules.
    a. small
    b. large
    c. unknown

20. We know that atoms of the same _____ can come together and atoms of different _____ can come together as well to form molecules.
    a. weight, weights
    b. team, teams
    c. element, elements

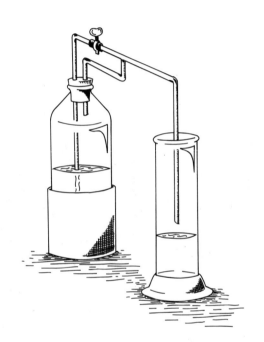

Unit Three
The Nature of Chemistry

Matter is a part of God's creation and it is subject to certain rules. Just like God has rules for people, the Bible tells us that He has rules for all of creation. In this unit we are going to see how different kinds of chemicals behave — how they act and how they react. Chemists have figured out some ways of describing these behaviors and some standard ways of naming things. Understanding these rules of behavior and the way things are named is helpful in studying chemistry because it allows everyone to communicate their ideas without being misunderstood. A chemist in Russia can look at an experiment done in the United States and understand it, even if he or she doesn't know the English language. This is because the words used in chemistry, including the names of the compounds and elements, the formulas, and the representation of the reactions, are pretty much the same in any language.

Additional Notes

Upon completing unit 3, the student should understand:

- The ways that atoms bond together
- Some of the standard ways to represent chemical compounds
- How chemicals react
- The chemistry of acids, bases, and salts

Unit 3 Vocabulary Words

- chemical bond
- ionic bond
- covalent bond
- chemical formula
- chemical name
- chemical nomenclature
- binary
- binary compound
- chemical reaction
- reactants
- products
- equations
- acids
- bases
- salts

Materials Needed for This Unit

- salt (regular table salt)
- coffee filter
- funnel
- two clear glass jars or drinking cups
- aluminum pie pan

Unit Three: The Nature of Chemistry

- water
- measuring cup
- one Alka-Seltzer tablet
- 3x5 index cards
- element cards that have already been started from lessons 4 and 8.
- pencil
- 4 tablespoons of baking soda (not baking powder)
- vinegar (any type will work — white distilled may be best)
- glass jar that will hold about 8 ounces of liquid
- tablespoon
- measuring cup
- bowl or pie pan
- one raw egg
- glass jar that will hold about 16 ounces or 500 milliliters
- safety glasses and smock

Additional Notes

Lesson 11
CHEMICAL BONDS

Teaching Time:
Keeping an Eye on Ionic Bonds

When two or more atoms join together to make a molecule or a compound, the joined atoms have to hold together. The way they stick together is by means of a chemical bond. A **chemical bond** is a very strong force between atoms that holds them together. Electrons in one atom are attracted to the protons in another atom, and this attractive electrical force forms a bond — sort of like two magnets being attracted to stick together. There are actually five types of chemicals bonds. In this book we will discuss two: an ionic bond in this lesson and a covalent bond in the next lesson.

◆ **Name It!**
<u>chemical bond</u>
A very strong force between atoms that holds them together.

<u>ionic bond</u>
A bond that occurs when one or more electrons from one atom is transferred to another atom.

Ionic Bond

Ionic bonds are formed between a metal compound and a non-metal compound. An **ionic bond** occurs when one or more

Additional Notes

electrons from one atom is transferred to another atom. The simplest example is the ionic bond between sodium (a metal) and chloride (a non-metal) in NaCl, commonly known as table salt. The sodium atom (atomic number 11) has 11 protons. This means it also has 11 electrons to balance off the charge. All of the 11 electrons are found in the shells around the nucleus. In the shell (outer shell) farthest away from the nucleus, there is only one lonesome electron. This electron is pretty far away from the sodium nucleus and so it is easily attracted to the nucleus of some other atom, such as chlorine.

Chlorine (atomic number 17) has 17 protons and 17 electrons to balance its charge. All 17 electrons are in shells around its nucleus. It has 7 of its electrons in its outer shell and would love to have 8 electrons to make it more stable. So when a sodium atom bumps into a chlorine atom, the lone electron in sodium's outer shell leaves and joins the outer shell in chlorine to make the chlorine more stable. This forms what is called an ionic bond between Na and Cl, holding the NaCl compound together. Although stable and bonded to chlorine, the sodium now has 10 electrons and is therefore a positively charged atom ($Na+$). Likewise, the chlorine bonded to sodium is stable since it has a full outer shell, but because it has the extra electron, giving a total of 18, it has a negative charge ($Cl-$). Both the chlorine and sodium atoms are now called ions. We will talk more about these ions in the lesson on salts (lesson 18).

Review It

1. A _____ _____ is a very

    strong force between atoms that holds them together.

2. An _____ bond occurs when one or more

    electrons from one atom are transferred to another atom.

Lesson 11: Chemical Bonds

3. There are actually _____ different types of chemicals bonds.

4. Electrons in one atom are attracted to the _____ in another atom, and this attractive electrical force forms a bond.

5. The bond between Na and Cl that holds the NaCl compound together is an _____ bond.

Hands-On:
Filtering Salt Water

When salt (NaCl) is in water, it dissociates and the salt grains disappear. This means that the ions of Na+ and the ions of Cl- temporarily come apart. This explains how the salt water was able to pass through the coffee filter that was used to separate the salt and sand in lesson 3.

Equipment Needed

- 2 teaspoons of salt (regular table salt)
- coffee filter
- funnel that will hold the filter in place
- two clear glass jars or drinking cups
- aluminum pie pan
- 100 milliliters of water
- measuring cup

Additional Notes

Additional Notes

Activity

1. Place the salt into one of the glass containers.

2. Measure and add 100 milliliters of water to the container and stir vigorously for about one minute.

3. Place the coffee filter into the funnel.

4. Place the funnel into the other glass container.

5. Slowly pour the contents of the bowl into the filter-lined funnel.

6. Allow the water to filter into the glass container.

7. Place 1 teaspoon of the liquid into a pie pan.

8. Keep the pie pan containing the liquid for a few days until the water has evaporated. Remember to come back and answer the questions that follow.

Think about It

1. When the salt was dissolved in the water, did the water still look clear?

   _____

   _____

Lesson 11: Chemical Bonds

2. Can you explain how the salt was able to go through the filter?

　_____

　_____

3. After the water evaporated, did you see any salt in the container?

　_____

　_____

4. Does the salt look the same as it did before? Can you explain this?

　_____

　_____

Additional Notes

Christian Kids Explore Chemistry

✝ **Scripture**
O Lord, our Lord, how majestic is your name in all the earth! (Psalm 8:1)

👁 **Discovery Zone**
The diagnosis of many illnesses is made possible by the analysis of chemicals, such as sodium, in the blood. Observing changes in blood chemistry helps doctors track down problems.

Hands-On: (Easier Alternative)
Clean up the Water

Did you know that we get our drinking water from rivers, streams, and underground wells? The water often contains many things that we really don't want to drink. This means that the water must be purified or filtered first. This removes the unwanted things, including certain chemicals. In this word find puzzle, we are going to clean up the water by finding and removing the things in the word list.

```
K  C  A  L  C  I  U  M  E  M
S  A  N  D  D  R  I  S  H  A
S  W  O  R  M  S  G  A  R  G
S  O  D  I  U  M  I  L  H  N
E  U  D  R  S  U  E  L  L  E
A  N  G  I  F  G  G  U  B  S
W  C  R  A  U  D  K  S  U  I
C  H  L  O  R  I  N  E  G  U
E  D  I  R  T  G  T  H  S  M
D  L  H  E  S  N  A  K  E  S
```

SAND	BUGS
DIRT	SNAKES
CHLORINE	WORMS
MAGNESIUM	SODIUM
CALCIUM	OIL

Lesson 12
MORE CHEMICAL BONDS

Teaching Time:
Coping with Covalent Bonds

Remember from the last lesson that a chemical bond is a very strong force between atoms that holds them together. Electrons in one atom are attracted to the protons in another atom, and this attractive force forms the bond. There are five different types of chemicals bonds, and we have already studied one, the ionic bond. We are now going to study a second type — the covalent bond.

Covalent Bonds

Most molecules are held together by covalent bonds. A **covalent bond** occurs between two atoms when these atoms share electrons. With ionic bonds, we saw how chlorine accepted a "gift" electron from sodium. In the case of covalent bonds, the electrons are merely shared and not given away. Remember, chlorine has seven electrons in its outer shell and needs one

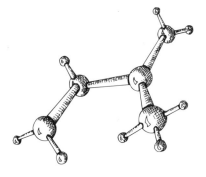

➲ **Name It!**
<u>covalent bond</u>
A bond that occurs between two atoms when these atoms share electrons.

Additional Notes

more electron to make it stable. So, one good way for that to happen is to get one from another chlorine atom. The other chlorine atom wants to be stable also, so it wants an electron also. The result is the two chlorine atoms share two electrons between them. Sharing is such a good deal (and stabilizing) that a bond is formed, called the covalent bond. In effect, each of the chlorine atoms now has eight electrons in its outer shell, but two of them are shared electrons. The result is Cl covalently bonded to Cl, and this forms a molecule of chlorine.

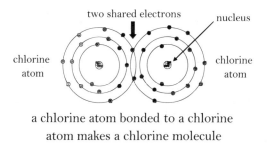

a chlorine atom bonded to a chlorine atom makes a chlorine molecule

Another example of a covalent bond is hydrogen gas. Hydrogen has only one electron, and to make it stable it needs two electrons in its outer shell. So, two hydrogen atoms share their two electrons with each other. This provides each hydrogen atom with two electrons in its outer shell.

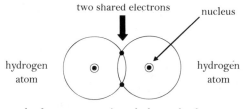

a hydrogen atom bonded to a hydrogen atom makes a hydrogen molecule

A hydrogen atom bonded to a hydrogen atom makes a hydrogen molecule.

Lesson 12: More Chemical Bonds

Review It

1. Most molecules are held together by _____ bonds.

2. In the case of covalent bonds, the electrons are merely _____, not given away.

3. Two chlorine atoms bond by sharing _____ electrons between them.

4. When one chlorine atom is covalently bonded to another chlorine atom, this forms a _____ of chlorine.

5. In effect, each of the chlorine atoms in a chlorine molecule now has _____ electrons in its outer shell.

Additional Notes

Hands-On:
Breaking Covalent Bonds

We will study chemical reactions in more detail in an upcoming lesson. Sometimes the chemical reactions result in chemical bonds being formed. However, in other reactions, chemical bonds are broken apart, and new ones are formed. There is a common product called Alka-Seltzer that many people take for colds and indigestion. If you have ever used it or seen someone

✝ **Scripture**
May God be gracious to us and bless us and make his face shine upon us. (Psalm 67:1)

👁 **Discovery Zone**
Oxygen makes up about 20% of the air in the atmosphere.

use it, you know it fizzes when dropped into water. Not very many people know what is really going on when that happens, but you will. The Alka-Seltzer tablet contains citric acid ($C_6H_8O_7$) and sodium bicarbonate ($NaHCO_3$). When the Alka-Seltzer is put into water, these ingredients dissolve and then react with each other. During the reaction, the covalent bonds are broken and carbon dioxide (CO_2) gas is formed and released (the bubbles), plus a citrate ion remains in the water.

Equipment Needed

- one Alka-Seltzer tablet
- water
- glass jar
- safety glasses and smock recommended

Activity

- Fill the glass jar with tap water.
- Add one Alka-Seltzer tablet to the jar of water.
- Observe the bubbling activity.

Think about It

1. How long did the reaction take?

   _____

   _____

Lesson 12: More Chemical Bonds

2. Was there more activity at first? Can you explain why?

   _____

   _____

Additional Notes

Lesson 13

FORMULAS

Teaching Time:
Fantastic Formulas

A **chemical formula** tells us what a compound is made of — the kinds and amounts of each element. One of the first things to note about formulas is the use of the chemical symbols to represent the elements. Up to now, when we've talked about the elements in our lessons, we provided the element name along with its chemical symbol, such as carbon (C). However, we could have just used the symbol C to represent the element. Did you realize that we have already been using a few chemical formulas in our lessons? We have used the formula for water — H_2O — and sodium chloride — NaCl. Let us look more closely at the water molecule with the formula for water, which is H_2O.

The formula H_2O means that there are two atoms of hydrogen bonded with one atom of oxygen. We know that there are two atoms of hydrogen because the subscript after the H is a 2. Whenever you see a subscript after an element symbol, it indicates the number of atoms involved. So, we also know from the

> ➡ **Name It!**
> <u>chemical formula</u>
> *A formula that tells us what a compound is made of — the kinds and amounts of each element.*

Additional Notes

formula that there is only one atom of oxygen because there is no subscript number after the O.

Sometimes more than one molecule is involved in a formula. When this occurs, the element is preceded by a number to indicate the appropriate number of molecules. The chemist signifies two molecules of H_2O by writing a 2 in front of the formula like this: $2H_2O$. Let's look at a larger molecule. The chemical formula for sucrose is $C_{12}H_{22}O_{11}$. What elements are represented by this formula? How many atoms of each element are bonded together? How many molecules are there represented? The answer is that sucrose has 12 carbon atoms, 22 hydrogen atoms, and 11 oxygen atoms. This represents one molecule of sucrose — a table sugar.

Review It

1. A _____ _____ tells us what a chemicals make up the compound.

2. Chemical _____ are used in formulas to represent the elements.

3. The formula H_2O means that there are _____ atoms of hydrogen bonded with _____ atom of oxygen.

4. The chemist signifies two molecules of H_2O by writing a 2 in _____ of the formula.

5. The chemical formula for sucrose is _____.

Lesson 13: Formulas

Hands-On:
Catch Up on Element Cards

In lesson 4 we started our element card collection, and in lesson 8 we did a catch-up. Since lesson 8 we have encountered more information about elements and we have learned some new ones. So, now is a good time to get caught up. Remember, anything we learn about the element, such as important formulas, can be added to the back of the cards. We will have one more element card catch-up in the next unit in lesson 20.

Equipment Needed

- pack of 3x5 index cards
- element cards that have already been started from lessons 4 and 8
- pencil

Activity

1. Go through the previous lessons and make a card for every element we have mentioned (except for the complete list of elements and abbreviations from lesson 4, of course). You should have quite a few.

2. Complete as much information as you can for each element. For some this may only be the element name and symbol.

Additional Notes

✝ **Scripture**
The Mighty One, God, the Lord, speaks and summons the earth from the rising of the sun to the place where it sets. (Psalm 50:1)

◉ **Discovery Zone**
Many of the medicines we take are made out of the chemicals found in plants.

3. Review the cards and think about what you know about each element.

4. Keep the cards in a card box or bound with a rubber band and remember to update them as we continue our study of chemistry.

Lesson 14

NAMING COMPOUNDS

Teaching Time:
Does Your Compound Have a Name?

There are many ways to refer to compounds. Take table salt for example. We can say its commonly used name — salt. We can refer to table salt by its chemical formula — NaCl — "Pass the NaCl, please!" We could also call it by its **chemical name**, sodium chloride — "French fries taste better with sodium chloride on them." Remember, God created the elements and their chemical properties.

Chemists and other scientists have developed a system of naming things in order to work with them. There are some rules to naming compounds. The system of rules and procedures are applied to what is called **chemical nomenclature**. This is done so that chemists all over the world can use the same name for a particular compound. An organization called the International Union of Pure and Applied Chemistry (or IUPAC) has set up this system of chemical nomenclature.

◯ **Name It!**
<u>chemical name</u>
The name given to a compound based on specific rules.

<u>chemical nomenclature</u>
The system of rules and procedures for naming chemical compounds.

119

◆ **Name It!**
<u>binary</u>
Two.

<u>binary compound</u>
A compound that contains two different elements.

Naming Compounds

Let's look at a compound we've already discussed — sodium chloride, or NaCl. Sodium chloride is an example of a type of compound known as a binary compound. **Binary** means two, and so a **binary compound** means a compound that contains two different elements such as Na and Cl. Table salt is the common name and sodium chloride is the chemical name. The first part of the name in the compound comes from the name of the first element, sodium. The second part of the name is chloride. The reason is a little tricky. Remember, this is a naming system based on the rules of chemistry. In this case, the stem part of the element name, *chlor-*, is used and the suffix *–ide* is added. You could actually use a table to find the ion name. The rules are sometimes complicated, but this is actually important and helpful in accurately describing the chemical formula. It is a language and, like the English language, it has rules. For compounds like sodium chloride, the rules are:

- Use the full name of the metal for the first name.
- Use only the stem of the non-metal as the second name.
- Add an *–ide* as a suffix to the second name.

Here is an example: K_3N. Using the chemical symbol table (found in lesson 4), we can determine that the K is potassium and the N is nitrogen. Using the rules, the first name is potassium and the second name is nitride. So the compound name is potassium nitride. That's not so hard. Here are some other examples:

BeO — Beryllium and oxygen compound is called beryllium oxide.

AlF_3 — Aluminum and fluoride compound is called aluminum fluoride.

There are many more naming rules for other compounds. Hopefully, you get the idea that chemists have a their own language when it comes to compounds in chemistry.

Lesson 14: Naming Compounds

Review It

1. Table salt has the chemical name of _____ _____.

2. _____ created the elements and their chemical properties.

3. _____ and other scientists have developed a system of naming things in order to work with them.

4. Sodium chloride is an example of a type of compound, called a _____ compound.

5. The naming system for compounds is based on the rules of _____.

Hands-On:
Naming Compounds

Knowing chemical compounds by their name can be easy, if you know your chemistry. Chemists who work with the same chemicals every day have come to know their names well and don't have to think about it. It's like knowing the names of your friends and relatives or the names of songs or sports teams. In this Hands-On, we are going to have fun determining the compound names based on the chemical formulas.

Additional Notes

Equipment Needed
None.

Activity
Figure out the name of the compound based on the chemical formula. You may need to refer to the list of chemical symbols listed in lesson 4 to figure out the symbol that is used for the element. Using the following list of examples of non-metal ion stems, complete the chart.

- oxygen   ox
- chlorine   chlor
- sulfur   sulf
- nitrogen   nitr
- fluorine   fluor

Compound Formula	Metal Element Name	Non-Metal Element Name	Non-Metal Element Stem	Compound Name
NaS_2				
$BaCl_2$				
K_2O	potassium	oxygen	ox	potassium oxide
K_3N				
$NaCl$				
Ca_3N_2				

Lesson 14: Naming Compounds

Think about It

1. If you see the name of a chemical compound on a label, do you think you might be able to determine what chemicals it is made of?

   _____

   _____

2. Now that you know how to determine some compound names from formulas, could you write a chemical formula based on the compound name? For example, calcium chloride? Try it.

   _____

   _____

✝ **Scripture**
I will praise you, O Lord, with all my heart; I will tell of all your wonders. (Psalm 9:1)

◉ **Discovery Zone**
Every compound has a scientific name — even water. Water is hydrogen and oxygen, or hydrogen oxide. Would you like to drink a glass of hydrogen oxide? How about a swim in some hydrogen oxide?

Lesson 15
REACTIONS

Teaching Time:
Rowdy Reactions

We learned that when two or more elements come together, either a compound or a mixture is formed. If the elements are only physically combined, it is a mixture. For example, air is a mixture of oxygen, nitrogen, carbon dioxide, and some other gases. So, if we took a sample of the air, we would find that there are many different gases all mixed together. When we take a breath, we actually inhale all of these gases into our lungs. However, it is only the oxygen that we keep and use. The other gases are sent back out when we exhale the air from our lungs. On the other hand, if elements are combined chemically, it is a compound. We have also learned that to be chemically combined means that a bond or connection is made between the elements that keeps them together under normal circumstances. The bond is the result of the two elements being connected together. The actual event when the chemicals come together and bond is called a **chemical reaction**. The resulting chemical bond is one of many things that can result from chemical reactions. Let's look at reactions further.

➡ **Name It!**
<u>chemical reaction</u>
The actual event when chemicals come together and bond.

> **➲ Name It!**
> <u>reactants</u>
> *The substances we begin with in a chemical reaction.*
>
> <u>products</u>
> *What remains after a chemical reaction takes place.*
>
> <u>equation</u>
> *The expression in writing of a chemical reaction.*

In a reaction, there are reactants and products. The **reactants** are the substances we begin with, and the **products** are what remain after the reaction takes place. What remains after a reaction can be a newly formed compound, such as when sodium and chlorine combine to form table salt, as well as leftover reactants, heat, and pure matter. Reactions can be violent and explosive. In the table salt reaction, a great deal of heat is given off.

Reactions are expressed in writing with **equations**. In a math equation, something happens on one side of an equal sign that must be equal to or balanced by the other side. For example, we know that $2 + 3 = 4 + 1$ is a balanced equation. Chemistry equations are written a little differently, but the idea is essentially the same. Let's look at the sodium and chlorine reaction in a chemical equation:

$$2Na + Cl_2 \rightarrow 2NaCl + Heat$$
sodium   chlorine   sodium chloride

This equation states that combining 2 "units" of sodium with a molecule of chlorine that is made of 2 chlorine atoms yields (or equals) 2 "units" of sodium chloride, or table salt, plus the heat that is given off. Understanding the balance is a little difficult for this lesson. Just appreciate the way that chemists can view and study the way things react by seeing the equation.

What about rusting steel or iron? Isn't that a chemical reaction? If you said yes, you are correct. The iron (Fe) reacts with the oxygen (O_2) in the air and water (H_2O) and produces iron hydroxide (rust). Let's take a look at that equation:

$$4Fe + 3O_2 + 6H_2O \rightarrow 4Fe(OH)_3 + Heat$$
iron   oxygen   water   iron hydroxide

Lesson 15: Reactions

This equation states that 4 "units" of iron combine with 3 "units" of oxygen and 6 "units" of water to yield 4 "units" of iron hydroxide (a type of rust) plus the heat that's given off.

Chemists are interested in many characteristics of chemical reactions. These characteristics include such things as how much heat is given off and how much time the reaction will take.

Review It

1. The actual events when the chemicals come together and bond is called a _____ _____.

2. A chemical _____ is one of many things that can result from chemical reactions.

3. The _____ are the substances we begin with in a reaction.

4. The _____ are what remains after the reaction takes place.

5. There are many _____ of reactions that chemists are interested in, such as how much heat is given off and how much time the reaction will take.

Additional Notes

Additional Notes

Hands-On:
Chemical Reaction

Things occur everyday that don't seem very special to the average person. But for a scientist, very few things can escape the curious mind. Just about every kitchen has two very reactive ingredients: vinegar and baking soda. Vinegar is actually a dilute solution of acetic acid (CH_3OOH). Baking soda is sodium bicarbonate ($NaHCO_3$). When the two ingredients are combined, a very interesting reaction occurs that changes the reactants (acetic acid and sodium bicarbonate) into new compounds (sodium acetate, carbon dioxide) and water. Here is the formula for the reaction.

$$CH_3OOH + NaHCO_3$$
acetic acid   sodium bicarbonate

$$\downarrow$$

$$NaO_2CCH_3 + CO_2 + H_2O$$
sodium acetate   carbon dioxide   water

Equipment Needed

- 4 tablespoons of baking soda
- vinegar (any type will work — white distilled may be best)
- glass jar that will hold about 8 ounces of liquid
- tablespoon
- measuring cup
- bowl or pie pan
- safety glasses and smock recommended

Lesson 15: Reactions

Activity

1. Scoop 4 tablespoons of baking soda into the glass jar.

2. Measure 100 milliliters of vinegar

3. Add the 100 milliliters of vinegar to the baking soda in the glass jar.

4. Observe the bubbling activity.

Think about It

1. How long did the reaction take?

   _____

2. Was there more activity at first? Can you explain why?

   _____

   _____

3. Were there any similarities between this reaction and the one involving the Alka-Seltzer in the Hands-On from lesson 12? Can you explain?

   _____

   _____

4. What were the bubbles?

   _____

✝ Scripture
The earth is the Lord's, and everything in it, the world, and all who live in it. (Psalm 24:1)

◉ Discovery Zone
A snake uses its tongue to detect very small amounts of chemicals in order to find other snakes. It can also use its chemical-detecting tongue to find lunch.

Lesson 16

Teaching Time:
Pay Attention to Acids

By the 1600s chemists figured out that compounds called acids and compounds called bases were very different compounds. They didn't even know the formulas for acids, but they did know something about their behavior:

- They taste sour in water.
- They corrode, or eat away, metals.
- They react with another type of compound called bases.

Some strong acids are very dangerous and are kept in a safe place in laboratories. They not only dissolve metals, but the dangerous ones can dissolve skin.

Much more is known today about the chemical makeup and properties of acids. The best definition that is used in modern chemistry says that an **acid** can donate or give away a proton (called a hydrogen ion) in a reaction. Let's think about that. We know from previous lessons that the definition of **ion** is an atom

◯ **Name It!**
<u>acid</u>
A chemical compound that donates or gives away a proton (called a hydrogen ion) in a reaction.

Additional Notes

with a charge (+ or -). That means that the atom has either gained or lost electrons. The atomic number of hydrogen is 1. Remember, this means it has one proton and one electron to balance it (keep it neutral). Therefore, when hydrogen is an acid, the hydrogen ion is a proton only. Let's look at a couple of examples. The first example is hydrochloric acid (HCl) in water.

$$HCl + H_2O \rightarrow H^+ + Cl^-$$

hydrochloric acid   water   hydrogen ion   chloride ion

We can see that HCl comes apart or dissociates in water to the hydrogen ion and to the chlorine ion. Now the chloride ion has an extra electron and we put a negative sign to show the extra electron. Another example is nitric acid in water.

$$HNO_3 + H_2O \rightarrow H^+ + NO_3^-$$

nitric acid   water   hydrogen ion   nitrate ion

Once again, the proton, or positive hydrogen ion, is produced, as well the negatively charged molecule, called nitrate.

Review It

1. By the 1600s chemists recognized that

    _____ and _____ are a

    different group of compounds.

Lesson 16: Acids

2. The best definition for an acid is that it can donate or give away a _____ in a reaction.

3. Acids corrode, or eat away, _____.

4. Acids react with another type of compound called _____.

5. The definition of _____ is an atom with a charge (+ or -).

Hands-On:
Hunting for Acids

Besides being found in chemistry laboratories, acids are common to many household products, foods, and over-the-counter medications. We should be able to recognize these when we see them and also remember what makes the compound an acid — it gives away a proton. We can go on a little field trip around the house and to the grocery store to locate some products that contain acid.

Equipment Needed

- pencil
- notebook

Additional Notes

Additional Notes

Activity

This chart contains the names of some common acid-containing products along with a little information that will help you locate them. Once you find each example, make a note on the chart. Try to find at least one example for each of the categories.

Name of Acid	Product Type or Hint	Name of Products	Notes (if any)
ascorbic acid	some foods and a particular vitamin		
phosphoric acid	soft drinks		
citric acid	shampoo and some canned goods		
salicylic acid	taken for headaches; also found in face cleansing pads		

Think about It

1. Why do you think there are acids in some foods?

   _____

   _____

Lesson 16: Acids

2. Did you ever think that a vitamin could be an acid?

   _____

   _____

3. When you think about these acids, are you imagining that they are giving up a proton?

   _____

   _____

4. Have you found any other products or thought of any other acids?

   _____

   _____

Scripture
Know that the Lord is God. It is he who made us, and we are his. (Psalm 100:3a)

Discovery Zone
Formic acid is the simplest acid. It is the same acid that causes the stinging and burning sensation when ants bite us.

Lesson 17

Teaching Time:
Beware of Bases

Before scientists understood the chemical composition and formulas for bases, they did know some facts about them:

- They taste bitter (DO NOT ever taste a base — it's VERY DANGEROUS).
- They are slippery to the touch.
- They dissolve fatty substances like grease.
- They react with acids.

Bases are caustic, which means they can cause severe skin irritation and damage. Chemists know how to handle them properly and always store them in safe places in the laboratory.

Modern chemists know that **bases** accept hydrogen ions in a reaction. This is exactly opposite from the way acids react. Do you think that bases and acids might react together since an acid donates protons and a base accepts protons? You are right, they do react. Here are a couple of examples. The first one is sodium

➜ **Name It!**
<u>bases</u>
A chemical compound that accepts or receives a proton (called a hydrogen ion) in a reaction.

Additional Notes

hydroxide in water. We can see that the sodium hydroxide comes apart in water and forms the sodium ion and the hydroxide ion.

$$\text{NaOH} + \text{H}_2\text{O} \rightarrow \text{Na}^+ + \text{OH}^-$$
sodium hydroxide base   water   sodium ion   hydroxide ion

The next example is ammonium hydroxide base reacting with hydrochloric acid, producing the salt ammonium chloride and water.

$$\text{NH}_4\text{OH} + \text{HCl} \rightarrow \text{NH}_4\text{Cl} + \text{H}_2\text{O}$$
ammonium hydroxide base   hydrochloric acid   ammonium chloride   water

Other common strong bases include lithium hydroxide, potassium hydroxide, and calcium hydroxide.

Review It

1. Bases taste _____.

2. Bases are _____ to the touch.

3. Bases dissolve fatty substances like _____.

4. Bases react with _____.

5. Bases _____ hydrogen ions in a reaction.

Lesson 17: Bases

Hands-On:
Hunting for Bases

In the last lesson we discussed that acids are common to many household products, foods, and over-the-counter medications. Bases are not. However, a few bases are used in everyday products and you should be able to recognize these when you see them. Also, remember what makes the compound a base — it accepts a proton during a reaction. Let's go on another field trip around the house or to the grocery store to locate and write down some products that contain bases. It is doubtful that you will find many different bases, but there are many products that contain ammonium hydroxide or sodium hydroxide.

Equipment Needed

- pencil
- notebook

Activity

The following chart will help you locate some products that contain the bases ammonium hydroxide or sodium hydroxide. Once you find the product, make a note in your notebook and then complete the chart with the missing information. Try to find at least three or four products. If you find others, write them in as well.

Additional Notes

✝ **Scripture**
I praise you because I am fearfully and wonderfully made. (Psalm 139:14a)

◉ **Discovery Zone**
Did you know that ordinary glass (like the windows in your house) are mostly made out of melted sand (silicon dioxide)?

Name of Base	Product Type or Hint	Name of Products	Notes (if any)
ammonium hydroxide	hair coloring		
ammonium hydroxide	cleaning agents		
ammonium hydroxide			
sodium hydroxide	oven cleaner		

Think about It

1. Is there anything that seems common to the product types?

   _____

   _____

2. When you think about these bases, are you imagining that they accept protons in a reaction?

   _____

   _____

Lesson 17: Bases

3. Did you find any other products containing bases?

_____

_____

Lesson 18

Teaching Time:
Salty Salts

When you think of salts, the first thing that may come to mind is the salt at home in the salt shaker. We've used table salt in many examples in our lessons. Such salt really is classified as a salt in the chemical sense — but, just why is it considered a salt? Before we find out, let's consider some other salts that we are familiar with.

One obvious example is the salt water that fills the oceans of the world. If you have ever been to the ocean, you may have tasted the salt in the water. That's the way God made oceans. Many other bodies of water, like rivers, streams, and lakes, are filled with fresh water — meaning they do not contain salt (at least not enough to taste). Tin fluoride (SnF_2) is a salt made in the laboratory by chemists and is used in toothpaste to prevent cavities. Another place we find salts is in our bodies and in other living organisms. Living things can contain sodium chloride as well as other types of salts that make the organism function properly. Let's take a look at the chemistry of salts.

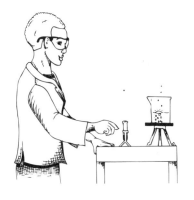

> **Name It!**
> <u>salt</u>
> *One of the products of a reaction between an acid and a base.*

Chemistry of Salts

Salts can be formed by a chemical reaction. When you combine an acid and a base, a chemical reaction occurs and you get two new products, water and **salt**. Remember, salts are ionic compounds, and ionic bonds hold them together. Ionic bonds are not as strong as covalent bonds and come apart easily in water. For example, NaCl dissolves in water to form the Na^+ ion and the Cl^- ion.

When an acid and a base react, the resulting product is a salt. If we add hydrochloric acid (HCl) to potassium hydroxide (KOH), the result is potassium chloride and water. Take a look!

$$HCl + KOH \rightarrow KCl + H_2O$$

hydrochloric acid — potassium hydroxide — potassium chloride — water

Many Salts Occur in Nature

NaCl, table salt, is found in salt mines. Sodium chloride is very important in the human body. One use is to make stomach acid (known as hydrochloric acid) for digestion. NaCl is also used in the brain's nerve cells. Both sodium nitrate ($NaNO_3$) and potassium nitrate (KNO_3) are found in natural deposits in the ground. Potassium nitrate is used to make gunpowder. Sodium nitrate is used for fertilizers. Calcium carbonate ($CaCO_3$) is found in chalk and limestone. Calcium carbonate is also the main ingredient found in antacids.

Review It

1. The oceans of the world are filled with

   _____.

Lesson 18: Salts

2. _____ (SnF$_2$) is a salt made in the laboratory by chemists and used in toothpaste to prevent cavities.

3. _____ _____ can have sodium chloride as well as other types of salts that make the organism function properly.

4. When an _____ and a _____ react, the resulting product is a salt.

5. A salt called _____ _____ is found in chalk and limestone.

Additional Notes

Hands-On:
Dissolving Calcium Carbonate with Acid

For this activity, we are going to put an acid to work in an unusual reaction. Don't worry, we are going to use a very weak acid — one that is often used in food preparation. The eggs of birds are made with a very hard shell. This shell is actually made of a compound called calcium carbonate (CaCO$_3$). We know acids will react with this compound, so we will see exactly what happens to an egg when it meets some vinegar (which you may remember is acetic acid).

Additional Notes

Equipment Needed

- one raw egg in its shell (and no cracks!)
- about 400 milliliters of vinegar (white distilled works best)
- glass jar that will hold about 16 ounces, or 500 milliliters
- safety glasses and smock recommended

Activity

1. Put the uncracked egg in the shell in a glass jar. (Be careful not to crack the egg shell. Cracks will affect the outcome of the experiment.)

2. Add about 400 milliliters of vinegar to the jar and do not put a lid on the jar.

3. Let the egg stay in the vinegar for 24 hours.

4. Take a look at the egg every few hours to observe its appearance.

5. After 24 hours has passed, carefully pour the vinegar down the drain and run some water over the egg to rinse it.

6. Remove the egg (be very careful) and gently dry it off.

7. Observe.

8. Use a toothpick or fork to open the membrane.

Lesson 18: Salts

Think about It

1. What did you observe during the 24-hour period whenever you took a look? Were there any bubbles? What do you think the bubbles were?

   _____

   _____

2. How did the egg look before and after the vinegar bath?

   _____

   _____

3. Describe the egg after the reaction.

   _____

   _____

4. What happened to the calcium carbonate?

   _____

   _____

✝ **Scripture**
Love the Lord your God with all your heart and with all your soul and with all your mind. (Matthew 22:37)

⚛ **Discovery Zone**
We taste salt on the tip of our tongue. Try it!

Unit Three Wrap-Up
Show What You Know!

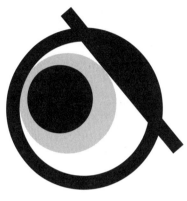

1. A _____ is a very strong force between atoms that holds them together.
    a. chemical bond
    b. light saber
    c. nuclear particle

2. A(n) _____ bond occurs when one or more electrons from one atom are transferred to another atom.
    a. covalent
    b. ionic
    c. special

3. There are actually _____ different types of chemicals bonds
    a. two
    b. hundreds of
    c. five

4. Electrons in one atom are attracted to the _____ in another atom and this attractive electrical force forms a bond.
    a. neutrons
    b. protons
    c. food

Study Notes

Study Notes

5. The bond between Na and Cl that holds the NaCl compound together is _____ bond.
   a. an ionic
   b. a bionic
   c. a covalent

6. In the case of covalent bonds, the electrons are merely _____, and not given away.
   a. sold
   b. shared
   c. destroyed

7. Two chlorine atoms bond by sharing _____ electrons between them.
   a. two
   b. four
   c. a dozen

8. When one chlorine atom is covalently bonded to another chlorine atom, this forms a _____ of chlorine.
   a. mass
   b. molecule
   c. bottle

9. A _____ tells us what chemicals make up the compound.
   a. telephone message
   b. chemical formula
   c. chemical reaction

10. Chemical _____ are used in formulas to represent the elements.
    a. compounds
    b. symbols
    c. factories

Unit Three Wrap-Up

11. The formula H_2O means that there are _____ atom(s) of hydrogen bonded with _____ atom(s) of oxygen.
    a. too many, too few
    b. one, two
    c. two, one

12. The chemist signifies two molecules of H_2O by writing a 2 in _____ of the formula.
    a. front
    b. back
    c. parentheses

13. Table salt has the chemical name of _____.
    a. sodium nitrate
    b. sodium chloride
    c. Benjamin Franklin

14. Remember, _____ created the elements and their chemical properties.
    a. scientists
    b. squirrels
    c. God

15. _____ and other scientists have developed a system of naming things in order to work with them.
    a. Chemists
    b. Librarians
    c. Hockey teams

Study Notes

Study Notes

16. Sodium chloride is an example of a type of compound, called a _____ compound.
    a. scarry
    b. binary
    c. fundamental

17. The actual event when the chemicals come together and bond is called a _____.
    a. birthday party
    b. chemical reaction
    c. chemical equation

18. A chemical _____ is one of many things that can result from chemical reactions.
    a. bond
    b. nucleus
    c. clearance sale

19. The _____ are the substances we begin with in a reaction.
    a. products
    b. dirty socks
    c. reactants

20. The _____ are what remains after the reaction takes place.
    a. products
    b. leftovers
    c. reactants

21. The best definition for an acid is that it can donate or give away a _____ in a reaction.
    a. prize
    b. proton
    c. neutron

Unit Three Wrap-Up

22. Acids corrode, or eat away, _____.
    a. metals
    b. plastics
    c. ice cream sandwiches

23. Acids react with another type of compound called _____.
    a. bases
    b. baseballs
    c. mixtures

24. The definition of _____ is an atom with a charge (+ or -).
    a. acid
    b. ion
    c. fun

25. Bases are _____ to the touch.
    a. slippery
    b. rough
    c. hot

26. Bases _____ hydrogen ions in a reaction.
    a. lose
    b. gain
    c. think about

27. The oceans of the world are filled with _____.
    a. monsters
    b. salt
    c. acid

Study Notes

Study Notes

28. Tin fluoride (SnF_2) is a salt made in the laboratory by chemists and is used in toothpaste to _____.
    a. prevent cavities
    b. cause cavities
    c. freshen breath

29. _____ can have sodium chloride, as well as other types of salts that make the organism function properly.
    a. Expensive clothes
    b. Fossil rocks
    c. Living things

30. A salt called _____ is found in chalk and limestone.
    a. calcium carbonate
    b. table salt
    c. sodium chloride

Unit Four
States of Matter

We now know a little about what matter is made of and how it acts under certain conditions, but there is something else we should explore. Matter can change its state, meaning it can be a solid, liquid, or gas. Even when the state of matter changes, it remains the same chemically; physically, it's in a different state.

Additional Notes

Upon completing unit 4, the student should understand:

- The three states of matter
- Two very important gas laws
- How states of matter are changed from one to another
- How and why things dissolve

Unit 4 Vocabulary Words

- solids
- liquids
- gas
- states of matter
- state change
- melting point
- freezing point
- boiling point
- solution
- solvent
- solute
- dilute solution
- saturated solution

Materials Needed for This Unit

- measuring cup with metric markings (milliliters or ml) that will measure at least 500 milliliters
- water
- salt
- sugar
- three rocks approximately the size of a ping-pong or golf ball
- laundry marking pen or crayons

- 3x5 index cards
- element cards that have already been started from lessons 4 and 8
- pencil
- small glass bottle (such as a Perrier water bottle) with a narrow neck (don't use plastic)
- two balloons
- a 2-quart saucepan or bowl
- six paper cups
- measuring spoon
- table salt
- thermometer that can measure the temperature of the freezer (optional)
- paper adhesive labels
- 1 cup of table sugar
- glass measuring cup
- safety goggles and lab smock

Lesson 19
SOLIDS AND LIQUIDS

Teaching Time:
Slow Solids and Lively Liquids

Did you know that molecules are always in motion? You might think they just rest quietly, but actually they are always moving around. Just how much molecules move depends on the amount of energy they have. The more energy they have, the more they move around. This idea of molecules moving around is important in explaining the difference between solids and liquids. Do you know the difference between a solid and a liquid? A liquid can be poured from one container to another, but a solid cannot. Let us look in more detail about the differences between solids and liquids.

➲ **Name It!**
<u>solid</u>
Any kind of matter that has a definite shape.

Solids

Any kind of matter that has a definite shape is a **solid**. Definite shape means that the shape doesn't change. Consider a piece of

161

> **Name It!**
> <u>liquid</u>
> *A state of matter in which the substance flows (like water), has a constant volume, and takes on the shape of its container.*

gold. It has a definite shape. If it is a piece of jewelry, it may be shaped like a ring, and when you place it on a finger, it keeps its shape. Can you name some other examples of matter that have definite shapes? It shouldn't be too hard to do since there are thousands of examples. Another important characteristic of solids is that they have definite volume. Volume is the amount of space something occupies or how much space there is. Let's think about a brick — the kind you might find in a building or a sidewalk. We can measure its length (7 inches); we can measure its height (2 inches); and we can measure its width (3 inches). By multiplying these three dimensions, we can figure out the volume: 7 x 2 x 3 = 42.

This means that the volume of the brick is 42 cubic inches of volume. Sometimes we represent volume using a metric system of measurement, which would result in the volume being described in milliliters instead of cubic inches, but it is still the volume. So solids are characterized by their definite shape and definite volume. Just remember that even if something is solid and keeps its shape, the molecules that it is made of are still moving, even if they are only moving a little.

Liquids

We said that the molecules in all matter move around. In solids, they move very little and that explains why the solid has a definite shape. In liquids, the molecules move much faster because they have more energy. This is why **liquids** don't have a definite shape. Liquids can take on different shapes depending on the shape of the container, but liquids do have a definite volume, and the volume can be measured. Let's look at liquid water for example. If we put some water into a measuring cup, we are able to look at the marks on the side of the cup and read the volume. This reading represents the exact volume of the liquid water. Try it. The volume is definite, but the shape is not definite. Let's say the volume of water is exactly 8 ounces. In the measuring cup, the water takes on the shape of the meas-

Lesson 19: Solids and Liquids

uring cup. If we pour the water from the cup into a bowl, the water takes on the shape of the bowl. If you put the 8 ounces of water in a flower vase, the water takes the shape of the vase. Even though the shape changes, the amount of liquid obviously stays the same. So, liquids have definite volume but indefinite shape. In lesson 22, we will learn more about the energy changes that can take place between the solids, liquids, and the "goofy gases."

Additional Notes

Review It

1. Molecules are in _____.

2. Any kind of matter that has a definite shape and definite volume is a _____.

3. In liquids, the _____ move much more often because they have more energy.

4. Liquids have an indefinite _____ but a definite _____.

5. Molecules move more when they have more _____.

Additional Notes

Hands-On:
Determining the Volume of a Solid

In this lesson we emphasized that one important characteristic of solid matter is definite volume. We could easily measure a brick and calculate its volume, but not every object is that easy. For example, a sphere, such as a golf ball, is round, so the calculation is a little different, but it can be calculated using a special formula. However, if we wanted to know the volume of something like a rock that has an unusual shape, the calculation could get complicated. Even if the shape of the rock is unusual, it still is solid and therefore has a definite shape. In this activity, we are going measure the volume of rocks to learn how to determine volume of unusually shaped objects. You may want to refer back to lesson 2 and review measuring — especially the discussion about interpolating.

Equipment Needed

- measuring cup with metric markings (milliliters or ml) that will measure at least 500 milliliters.
- water
- three rocks approximately the size of a ping-pong or golf ball
- laundry marking pen or crayons

Activity

1. Using the crayon or laundry marker, mark each rock with a different letter (A, B, and C).

Lesson 19: Solids and Liquids

Rock Sample	Water-Level Measurement without Rock	Water-Level Measurement with Rock	Volume of Rock Sample (Subtract 300 from the measurement with rock)
rock A	300 ml		
rock B	300 ml		
rock C	300 ml		
other			

2. Fill the measuring cup with exactly 300 ml of water.

3. Add the rock marked A; then record the measuring cup reading on the chart above. Remember from lesson 2, it is sometimes necessary to interpolate (or read between the lines) when measuring.

4. Remove rock A, letting all the water drip back into the measuring cup.

5. Check to be sure the water level returns to the 300 ml mark. If it doesn't, then carefully add a little more water until it is exactly 300 ml.

6. Repeat the steps with the other rocks, recording the readings on the chart.

7. Complete the calculation indicated on the chart.

Scripture
There is a mine for silver and a place where gold is refined. Iron is taken from the earth, and copper is smelted from ore. (Job 28:1-2)

Discovery Zone
Water weighs about one pound per pint. So, if you want to quickly gain a pound (temporarily), just drink a pint of water.

Additional Notes

Think about It

1. Were you surprised at how easy it is to determine the volume of a solid that has an unusual shape?

   _____

   _____

2. Could this technique be used to figure out the volume of a person? Explain the way you would measure the volume of a person.

   _____

   _____

Lesson 20

Teaching Time:
Goofy Gases

Remember that we said that the molecules in solids move — but not very fast. We learned that molecules in liquids have more energy and move faster than molecules in solids. Well, the molecules in gases move the fastest. This is because molecules in a **gas** have a lot of energy. The slow-moving molecules in solids allow them to keep their shape. The molecules in a liquid have more energy, so the liquid can be poured, but it still stays inside its container. The molecules in a gas have a great deal of energy and move very fast. As a result, gases tend to spread out; they don't stay in one place very long. Gases do not have a definite shape or volume, but they will stay inside a container as long as it is closed tightly.

Can you think of any containers that have gas inside of them? One very common container is a balloon. Sometimes we blow air into a balloon to fill it up. This air is a mixture of many gases in our atmosphere, such as oxygen (O_2), nitrogen (N), and carbon dioxide (CO_2). Or people fill balloons with helium (He). This gas

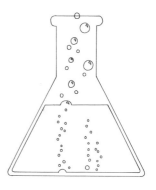

➲ Name It!
<u>Gas</u>
A state of matter in which the substance is airlike and does not have a definite shape or a definite volume.

is very light compared to the normal air mixture and that's why it rises. If you tried to put helium gas in a cup it would escape into the air. Gases behave nicely inside a balloon, but those gas molecules have a lot of energy and want out. See what happens if you take a balloon and put a tiny hole in it. The molecules soon escape from the hole into the air.

When we talk about a gas, we are referring to a substance that is a gas at normal room temperature. Besides helium, oxygen, nitrogen, and carbon dioxide, there are many other elements that are gases at room temperature. Can you think of any? Of course there is hydrogen (H) and all the noble gases that we mentioned when we looked at the periodic table of the elements. There are many gases that we will be talking about when we study the organic chemistry in the next unit. These gases are dangerous and explosive.

Review It

1. The molecules in a gas have a lot of _____.

2. _____ tend to spread out; they don't stay in one place very long.

3. Gases do not have a definite _____.

4. The air is a mixture of many gases in our atmosphere such as _____ (O_2), _____ (N), and _____ _____ (CO_2).

5. Helium (He) is a gas that is very _____ compared to the normal air mixture, and that's why it rises.

Lesson 20: Gases

Hands-On:
Catch Up on Element Cards

It's time to catch up on the element cards for this unit. Check out your cards and add any information that may be helpful in understanding the elements. Boiling point, melting point, and freezing point may be interesting and helpful facts to add. Also, we've been talking about gases in this unit. Using the Internet, science books, or encyclopedia, look up the noble gases that we first discussed in lesson 9, and see how much information you can find on them.

Equipment Needed

- pack of 3x5 index cards
- element cards that have already been started from lessons 4 and 8
- pencil

Activity

1. Add new elements that we have studied and update the ones you already have.

2. Complete as much information as you can for each element. For some this may only be the element name and symbol.

3. Review the cards and think about what you know about each element.

Additional Notes

✝ **Scripture**
Give thanks to the Lord, for he is good; his love endures forever. (Psalm 107:1)

◉ **Discovery Zone**
One of the most important things the element calcium does in our bodies is to help our heart work correctly.

4. Keep the cards in a card box or bound with a rubber band and remember to update them as we continue our study of chemistry.

Lesson 21

GAS LAWS

Teaching Time:
The Gas Police

What do we mean by gas laws? Do gas molecules really obey them? Yes, gas molecules really do obey these laws, but the molecules actually do not have any other choice; they are simply created that way by God. Gas laws and other laws in chemistry are an example of the order that God has created in the physical world of matter. In this lesson, we will discuss two gas laws — Boyle's law and Charles's law. These laws have to do with the temperature, volume, and pressure of a gas. **Pressure** is a word that is used to mean some amount of force that is applied to something. For example, you can put pressure on a certain area of your arm by squeezing it, and the amount of pressure on your arm could be measured. Or, when you fill a bicycle tire, it is important to know the pressure reading because too much air can make the tire explode. The same is true of car tires and even balloons. When we talk about a gas, we say that there is a specific amount of pressure placed on the gas. In other words, the gas is under pressure.

Additional Notes

Boyle's Law

In 1662, a British chemist and physicist named Robert Boyle discovered that if gas is put under a great amount of pressure, the volume of the gas would decrease as long as the temperature of the gas stayed the same. So, when much pressure is placed on gas, it can fit into a smaller space or volume. Let us say that you have a bottle filled with 2 liters of helium and it is has a pressure of 20 pounds per square inch (PSI). If the pressure is increased to 40 PSI, the gas will squeeze into a smaller amount of space — one liter. If you put the gas under 80 PSI of pressure, it will occupy a space of only one-half liter. So, Boyle's law says that if the pressure is increased, the volume will decrease.

Charles's Law

In 1787, a French scientist named Jacques Charles figured out how temperature affects the volume of a gas. Charles's law says that as the temperature of the gas is increased, the volume of the gas increases also. If our balloon contained 2 liters of helium (or any gas) at 100°K and the temperature is then doubled to 200°K, the volume of the gas in the balloon would be doubled to 4 liters. If we increase the temperature to 400°K, the volume of gas would expand to 8 liters. Of course, the balloon would have to withstand a pretty high temperature (but you get the idea). So, Charles's law says if the temperature is increased, the volume will increase.

(NOTE: Kelvin temperature [K] is a measurement of absolute temperatures. It is a way for scientists to measure temperature other than Celsius or Fahrenheit.)

Lesson 21: Gas Laws

Review It

1. Gas laws and other laws in chemistry are an example of the order that God has _____ in the physical world of matter.

2. _____ is a word that is used to mean the amount of force that is applied to something.

3. Boyle's law says if the pressure is _____, the volume will decrease.

4. Charles's law says if the temperature is _____, the volume will increase.

5. Gas molecules really do obey the _____ _____.

Hands-On:
Testing Charles's Gas Law

If what Jacques Charles said about gases is true, we should be able to demonstrate it. There are some hard ways to check this out and some easy ways. One easy way is to trap some gas in a container, add some heat, and see if the volume of gas

Additional Notes

increases or not. Whether it is a single element gas, such as oxygen, or a mixture of gases in the air (nitrogen, oxygen, and carbon dioxide), the gas laws still apply. By putting a lid on the container, we have essentially trapped the gases inside. So, if we use a balloon as a lid over the top of the container, the gases are trapped. The advantage to a balloon is that we can *see* the volume of gases increasing as the balloon fills when heat is applied and the temperature of the gas increases.

Equipment Needed

- small glass bottle with a narrow neck, such as a Perrier water bottle. (Don't use plastic.)
- balloon
- 2-quart saucepan or bowl
- water
- safety goggles and lab smock recommended

Activity

1. Place the glass bottle into the refrigerator and leave it there for an hour.

2. Using the hottest water possible from the sink faucet, fill the 2-quart pan or bowl about three-fourths full of the hot water and set aside.

3. Retrieve the glass bottle from the refrigerator and quickly place a balloon over the mouth of the bottle. Ensure that it is sealed tightly.

4. Carefully place the bottle with the balloon in the hot water. You can also carefully allow hot water to run over the lower part of the bottle.

Lesson 21: Gas Laws

5. Observe the balloon.

6. Change the hot water to cold water and observe the change in the balloon.

7. Place the bottle, with the balloon still attached, back into the refrigerator.

8. Observe after an hour.

Think about It

1. About how much did the balloon fill up when the bottle was placed into the hot water? Can you explain the change in the balloon?

   _____

   _____

2. Where did the air that filled the balloon come from?

   _____

   _____

3. Why do you think the bottle was first put into the refrigerator?

   _____

   _____

✝ Scripture
Great are the works of the Lord: they are pondered by all who delight in them. (Psalm 111:2)

◉ Discovery Zone
Diamonds are actually a pure form of carbon.

Lesson 22
STATE CHANGE

Teaching Time:
Some Statements about States

The difference between solids, liquids, and gases is really the difference in the amount of energy the molecules have. We know that the molecules in a liquid move much faster than the molecules in a solid, and the molecules in a gas move faster than the molecules in a liquid. So, if it is only a matter of energy level, what happens to a solid if we give it some energy? Wouldn't the molecules move faster? Yes! There are three states of matter: solid, liquid, and gas. Matter that is solid is said to be in a solid state. When it is liquid, it is in a liquid state. When it is a gas, it is in a gas state. When matter changes from one state to another, we call it a **state change**.

➲ Name It!
<u>state change</u>
When matter changes from one state to another.

◈ **Name It!**

melting point
The temperature at which a solid melts.

freezing point
The temperature at which a liquid freezes.

Melting Point — Solid to Liquid

If a solid is heated, the molecules receive energy and this makes them move faster. Heat is energy that can be put into matter. After heating a solid to a certain temperature, it melts and becomes a liquid. The temperature at which a solid melts is called the **melting point**. Water in the solid form (ice) melts at 32°F to the liquid form of water. Something like iron (Fe) melts at a much higher temperature, 2795°F. At that temperature, iron is a very hot liquid and it has a great deal of energy. If the temperature goes below 2795°F, the iron will become solid again. Aluminum is another metal solid with a high melting point — about 1220°F.

Freezing Point — Liquid to Solid

If the temperature of a liquid is lowered, heat (energy) is taken away from the molecules, causing them to move slower. After lowering the temperature to a certain point, the energy level is so low that the liquid freezes into a solid. The temperature at which the liquid freezes is called the **freezing point**. Another term for freezing point is solidification point. Water in its liquid form will freeze into solid ice at 32°F. It is also the point at which the solid water, the ice, will turn back into water. The freezing point and melting point of a substance are the same. It is the point at which the state will change to solid with a little less heat or to a liquid with a little more heat. We said the melting point of iron is 2795°F. Therefore, you could say that it is the freezing point as well because with a little less heat the iron begins to solidify again.

Boiling Point — Liquid to Gas

When even more heat is applied, liquid molecules get even more energy and move even faster. Eventually those molecules have enough energy to escape from the liquid and move into the air as a gas. It may be hard to imagine, but even iron can be turned into a gas if enough heat is applied. Those molecules would get so

Lesson 22: State Change

much energy, they would just fly away into the air. The temperature at which a liquid becomes a gas is called the **boiling point**. The boiling point for water is 212°F. This means that as soon as some of the water molecules reach that temperature they become water vapor. We know that iron is a solid. We also know that iron will melt at 2795°F. Do you think iron could actually turn into a gas? Of course it can. It takes a very powerful heat source, but by heating iron to 4982°F, it becomes a gas and floats off into the air. So, we say the boiling point for iron is 4982°F.

> ◯ Name It!
> **boiling point**
> *The temperature at which a liquid becomes a gas.*

Review It

1. The difference between solids, liquids, and gases is the difference in the amount of _____ the molecules have.

2. If a solid is heated, the molecules are getting energy to move _____. Heat is _____ that can be put into matter.

3. The temperature at which the solid melts is called the _____ point.

4. The temperature at which the liquid freezes is called the _____ point.

5. The temperature at which the liquid becomes a gas is called the _____ point.

Additional Notes

Hands-On: Evaluating the Freezing Point of NaCl in Water

Every substance has a solidification point (freezing point), a melting point, and a boiling point. These are the temperatures at which the state will change between solid, liquid, and gas. These are some of the physical properties that we talked about in lesson 3. Pure water has a freezing point of 32°F. However, when the compound sodium chloride (table salt) is dissolved in water, the freezing point of the water is lowered, which means that it won't freeze at 32°F. The reason for the difference in freezing point is a little complicated, but it has to do with the molecular structure and interaction of the Na and Cl ions in the water. Sometimes when ice forms on streets and sidewalks, sodium chloride and other salts like calcium chloride are used to melt the ice and keep the surface from becoming slippery and dangerous. We will see this chemistry in action in this Hands-On.

Equipment Needed

- two paper cups
- measuring spoon
- measuring cup
- table salt
- thermometer that can measure the temperature of the freezer (optional)
- paper adhesive labels

Lesson 22: State Change

Activity

1. Label one paper cup "NaCl and H_2O" and label the other cup "H_2O Only."

2. Fill a measuring cup with 50 milliliters of water.

3. Pour the water into the "H_2O Only" paper cup.

4. Fill the measuring cup again with 50 milliliters of water.

5. Add 3 teaspoons of salt to the water in the measuring cup.

6. Using a spoon, stir vigorously for about two minutes or until the salt is almost completely dissolved in the water.

7. Pour the contents of the measuring cup into the "NaCl and H_2O" paper cup.

8. Place both of the cups in the freezer.

9. Place the thermometer anywhere inside the freezer.

10. Wait about four hours.

11. Read the temperature of the freezer (optional).

12. Remove the cups from the freezer and observe the contents.

13. Return the cups to the freezer, wait 24 hours, and examine the contents again.

Additional Notes

✝ **Scripture**
Shout for joy to the Lord, all the earth. (Psalm 100:1)

◉ **Discovery Zone**
Chemists who study analytical chemistry try to figure out what things are made of.

Think about It

1. Were you surprised that there were no differences in the condition of the contents of the cups after 24 hours?

   _____

   _____

2. What was the temperature of the freezer? Therefore, what was the temperature of the NaCl dissolved in water?

   _____

   _____

3. Do you think the water would freeze if less NaCl was in it? Try using 2 teaspoons, 1 teaspoon, and ½ teaspoon.

   _____

   _____

Lesson 23
SOLUTIONS

Teaching Time:
A Salute to Solutions

What do you think of when someone says the word *solution*? In chemistry, a **solution** means that two or more substances (either a compound or an element) are mixed very well together so that all the different atoms and molecules are evenly distributed.

There are two types of ingredients in a solution, the solvent and the solute. The **solvent** of the solution is the substance present in the solution in the greatest amount. The **solute** is the substance present in a lesser amount. We sometimes say the solute is dissolved in the solvent. For liquid/solid solutions, the liquid is the solvent and the solid substance is the solute. It is possible to have more than one solute in a solution. For example, in a sodium chloride/sucrose/water solution, water is the solvent and sodium chloride (table salt) and sucrose (sugar) are the solutes.

There are also gas/gas, gas/liquid, liquid/liquid, and solid/solid solutions. Do you think that a solid/solid solution sounds strange? One example of a solid/solid solution is sterling silver, which is made by combining the elements of copper

➲ **Name It!**
<u>solution</u>
Two or more substances (either a compound or an element) mixed very well together so that all the different atoms and molecules are evenly distributed.

<u>solvent</u>
The substance present in a solution in the greatest amount.

> **Name It!**
>
> <u>solute</u>
> *The substance present in a solution in a lesser amount.*
>
> <u>dilute solution</u>
> *A solution in which just a small amount of a solute is dissolved.*
>
> <u>saturated solution</u>
> *A solution of the greatest amount of solute that can be dissolved into a solvent at a given temperature.*

and silver. Silver is the solvent since it is present in the greatest amount and copper is the solute. An example of a gas/liquid solution is carbonated water. Water is the solvent and carbon dioxide gas is the solute. What kind of solution do you think soft drinks are? If you think it is a solid/gas/liquid solution, you are right.

There is another way to characterize solutions and that is by telling how much of the solute is present — in general terms. A **dilute solution** means that just a small amount of a solute is dissolved. Some amount of solute is added to a solvent and stirred a little, and it is dissolved. A **saturated solution** contains the greatest amount of solute that can be dissolved into a solvent at a given temperature.

Review It

1. A _____ means that two or more substances are mixed very well together so that all the different atoms and molecules are evenly distributed.

2. There are two types of ingredients in a solution, the _____ and the _____.

3. The solvent of the solution is the substance present in the solution in the _____ amount.

4. The solute (or solutes) is the substance present in a _____ amount.

Lesson 23: Solutions

5. Soft drinks are an example of a

_____/_____/

_____ solution.

Hands-On:
Preparing a Saturated Solution

Sugar solutions are important in the kitchen, in the laboratory, and in medicine. In the kitchen, there are a variety of syrups and other sugar-containing liquids. The laboratory relies on known concentrations of sugar solutions for experiments. If you have ever been in a hospital or watched a television program about hospitals, you've probably seen patients with an intravenous (IV) tube going into a vein in their arm. The tube comes from a bottle that is usually hanging on a pole beside the patient's bed. A variety of medicines can be in the bottle, but many times the clear liquid going into the patient is a sugar solution. The sugar can be glucose and is given to replace fluids and give the patient strength to get well. The amount of glucose varies (5%, 10%, or 20% glucose solution), but they are all made by dissolving the glucose (solute) into water (solvent). This means that a certain percentage of the solution in the bottle is glucose.

For this Hands-On, we will make a saturated sugar solution using sucrose (table sugar) and water.

Additional Notes

Additional Notes

Equipment Needed

- 1 cup (250 milliliters) of sucrose (table sugar)
- 100 milliliters of water
- glass measuring cup
- measuring tablespoon

Activity

1. Pour 100 milliliters of water into the measuring cup.

2. Add sugar, 1 tablespoon at a time, to the water. Stir each spoonful until completely dissolved.

3. After each tablespoon is added and stirred, observe the solution. If all the sugar crystals dissolve and the solution is clear, then the solution is not yet saturated. (Note: It may take quite a few tablespoons to get a saturated sucrose solution. The amount of sugar required may vary due to water hardness or temperature variation.)

4. When the crystals no longer dissolve — even after several minutes of stirring — the saturation point has been exceeded.

Think about It

1. How many tablespoons of sugar did it take to get to saturation?

_____

_____

Lesson 23: Solutions

2. What do you think will happen if you let the liquid evaporate? You could pour some into a pie pan or jar and see. This may take several days — be patient. Describe what remains in the cups.

_____

_____

Hands-On (Easier Alternative)
Which Is Which?
When salt (NaCl) is dissolved in water, the original shape of the salt grains is no longer visible. The same is true when sugar is dissolved in water. This would make it difficult to determine which was which based on appearance.

Equipment Needed

- four paper cups that are exactly alike
- table salt
- sugar

Activity

1. Fill each cup with 4 ounces of warm tap water.

2. In two of the cups, place 1 teaspoon of sugar.

3. In the other two cups, place 1 teaspoon of salt.

4. Stir all four cups until the salt and sugar are dissolved.

Additional Notes

✝ **Scripture**
May the glory of the Lord endure forever; may the Lord rejoice in his works. (Psalm 104:31)

◉ Discovery Zone
The ocean is really a giant solution. Water is the solvent and many salts are the solutes.

5. Mix up the cups so you don't know which has sugar and which has salt.

6. Examine each cup and try to determine which ones contain dissolved sugar and which contain the dissolved salt.

7. After trying to guess by looking, try smelling the solutions.

8. After smelling, try tasting the solutions. (Take a very small taste; you might want to spit it out.)

Think about It

1. Discuss the process of trying to figure out which was which. How did you do in guessing? This demonstrates that appearance isn't always a good way to determine what a substance is.

_____

_____

Unit Four Wrap-Up
Show What You Know!

1. Molecules in solids, liquids, or gases are always in _____.
    a. motion
    b. trouble
    c. atomic chaos

2. Any kind of matter that has a definite shape and definite volume is a _____.
    a. gas
    b. solid
    c. puzzle

3. In liquids, the _____ move much more often because they have more energy.
    a. molecules
    b. protons
    c. bugs

4. Liquids have an indefinite _____ and a definite _____.
    a. volume, shape
    b. problem, solution
    c. shape, volume

Study Notes

Study Notes

5. Molecules move more when they have more
   _____.
   a. space
   b. money
   c. energy

6. The molecules in a gas have a lot of
   _____.
   a. volume
   b. energy
   c. fun

7. _____ tend to spread out and don't stay in one place very long.
   a. Gases
   b. Cats
   c. Solids

8. Gas laws and other laws in chemistry are an example of the order that God has _____ in the physical world of matter.
   a. created
   b. learned
   c. forgotten

9. _____ is a word that is used to mean the amount of force that you apply to a specific area.
   a. Pressure
   b. Stress
   c. Punch

10. Boyle's law says if the pressure is _____, the volume will decrease.
    a. decreased
    b. increased
    c. released

Unit Four Wrap-Up

11. Charles's law says if the temperature is _____, the volume will increase.
    a. decreased
    b. increased
    c. cold

12. Gas molecules really do obey the _____.
    a. speed limit
    b. gas laws
    c. ten commandments

13. The difference between solids, liquids, and gases is really the difference in the amount of _____ the molecules have.
    a. money
    b. power
    c. energy

14. Heat is _____ that can be put into matter.
    a. temperature
    b. energy
    c. wasted

15. The temperature at which a solid melts is called the _____ point.
    a. final
    b. important
    c. melting

16. The temperature at which a liquid freezes is called the _____ point.
    a. freezing
    b. extreme
    c. good

Study Notes

Study Notes

17. The temperature at which a liquid becomes a gas is called the _____ point.
    a. gaseous
    b. boiling point
    c. your

18. A _____ means that two or more substances are mixed very well together so that all the different atoms and molecules are evenly distributed.
    a. solution
    b. mess
    c. compound

19. There are two types of ingredients in a solution: the _____ and the _____.
    a. important, unimportant
    b. solvent, solute
    c. liquid, solid

20. Soft drinks are a _____ / _____ / _____ solution.
    a. solid, liquid, gas
    b. gas, gas, gas
    c. liquid, liquid, gas

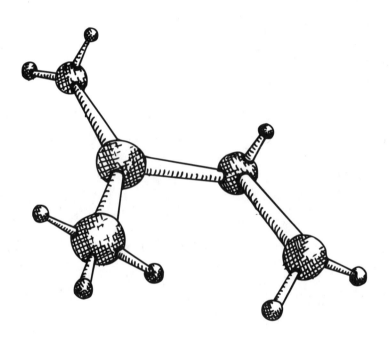

Unit Five
Organic Chemistry

Organic chemistry is a type of chemistry that deals with certain compounds that have the element of carbon in them. Just about every part of every *living* thing, whether plant or animal, is made of carbon-based compounds. Besides that, many fuels (such as gas for our vehicles and heating oil for our homes) are carbon compounds. Understanding this type of chemistry is important for biomedical scientists, the doctors that try to keep us healthy, and also the people who work in the petroleum or oil industry. Organic chemistry is the chemistry of God's world.

Additional Notes

Upon completing unit 5, the student should understand:

- The concept of hydrocarbon compounds
- The three main families of hydrocarbons
- The chemistry of the hydrocarbon derivative called alcohols
- The chemistry of the hydrocarbon derivative called esters
- The main molecules of biochemistry

Unit 5 Vocabulary Words

- hydrocarbons
- organic chemistry
- organic compounds
- alkanes
- alkenes
- alkynes
- alcohols
- OH group
- detoxified
- esters
- biochemistry
- monosaccharides
- polysaccharide

Materials Needed for This Unit

- glass jar with a lid that fits well
- 2 tablespoons of motor oil (used for cars or lawn mowers)
- 2 tablespoons of petroleum jelly
- water
- nine Styrofoam balls (2-inch diameter)
- 18 Styrofoam balls (1-inch diameter)
- round toothpicks

Unit Five: Organic Chemistry

- three clean plastic margarine or butter containers with lids
- isopropyl alcohol or rubbing alcohol (70% solution)
- thermometer that can measure the temperature of the freezer (optional)
- measuring cup
- crayons
- pencil
- safety glasses and smock

Additional Notes

Lesson 24
HYDROCARBONS

Teaching Time:
You Can't Hide From Hydrocarbons

By now, it should be easy to guess what hydrocarbons are. From the name, we can figure out that there must be some hydrogen present. We can also see the word carbon in the name, so there must be carbon present. This is exactly right. **Hydrocarbons** are a family of compounds that are made of various combinations and amounts of the element hydrogen and the element carbon. Hydrocarbons make up a type of chemistry called **organic chemistry** and the carbon compounds studied are called **organic compounds**.

Carbon can bond (connect) to other carbon atoms and form long chains, even connecting in ways that form rings. Each and every carbon atom can form four covalent bonds. That means that up to four other atoms can connect to it. You might think of carbon like a building block or a Lego piece with four connections.

➔ Name It!
<u>hydrocarbons</u>
A family of compounds that are made of various combinations and amounts of the element hydrogen and the element carbon.

<u>organic chemistry</u>
The study of hydrocarbons.

<u>organic compounds</u>
Carbon compounds.

207

Additional Notes

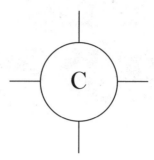

In previous lessons, we have seen some of the compounds that are formed with carbon, such as carbon dioxide or calcium carbonate. However, when carbon atoms bond with other carbon atoms and with hydrogen atoms, we have what is called an organic compound, a hydrocarbon. There are over six million organic compounds — that's a lot of organic compounds. Besides hydrocarbons, there are other major types of organic compounds. They are called derivatives of hydrocarbons. The derivatives of hydrocarbons include alcohols and esters, which we will talk about later in this unit.

You wouldn't think so many compounds could form from just carbon and hydrogen, but it's possible because the carbon atoms can connect in a long chain. The carbons can connect together in a couple of different ways, such as in a ring or commonly in a sequence called a chain. The simplest hydrocarbon compound is methane gas with the formula of CH_4. This is a pretty short chain with only one carbon. Let's first take a look at the methane molecule, showing the carbon atom with each of its four available covalent bonding sites filled with a hydrogen atom.

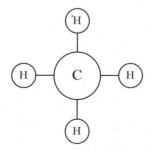

Lesson 24: Hydrocarbons

The carbon and each hydrogen atom that is bonded with each covalent bond share two electrons. Methane gas is sometimes used for fuel in furnaces.

A chain with only two carbons is ethane gas with the formula of C_2H_6. Take a look at how it looks.

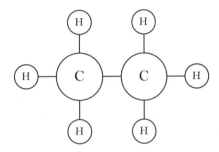

Can you count the number of bonds? If you said seven, you are right. Each line between the atoms represents a single bond where two electrons are shared. Instead of a hydrogen atom on every bonding site, ethane uses one site to connect to another carbon atom.

Other Examples of Hydrocarbons

Petroleum is a source of many different hydrocarbons. Petroleum is sometimes called crude oil. It is pumped out of the ground in the U.S., the Middle East, and other places in the world. You may have seen pictures of an oil well or even seen wells pumping away in fields. Petroleum can be processed in a petroleum refinery to separate the different hydrocarbons into a more pure form. There are some familiar hydrocarbon products that come from petroleum. These are natural gas, kerosene, and asphalt. Gasoline that you burn in a car is a mixture of hydrocarbon chains that can contain 5, 6, or 7 carbons atoms. Kerosene contains a mixture of hydrocarbon chains with 12, 13, 14, 15, or 16 carbon atoms. Kerosene is used in jet fuel and diesel fuel. Asphalt is a solid used to pave roads and

Additional Notes

Additional Notes

put on top of roofs. It contains hydrocarbons that have over 20 carbon atoms per chain. Another type of hydrocarbon is coal, which is a fuel source for industry. Some homes still burn coal as a heating fuel.

In the next lessons, we will look at the three main categories of hydrocarbons: alkanes (with single covalent bonds), alkenes (with double covalent bonds), and alkynes (with triple covalent bonds). We will also talk about the alcohols and esters.

Review It

1. _____ are a family of compounds that are made of various combinations and amounts of the element hydrogen and the element carbon.

2. Hydrocarbons make up a type of chemistry called _____ _____.

3. The simplest hydrocarbon compound is _____ gas with the formula CH_4.

4. There are some familiar hydrocarbon products that come from petroleum. These are natural gas, _____, and _____.

5. Carbon atoms have _____ available bonding sites.

Lesson 24: Hydrocarbons

Hands-On:
Floating Hydrocarbons

Liquid hydrocarbons have an interesting property. As a rule, they are lighter than water. We might think of oils (which are long chain hydrocarbons) as being thick and gooey. Since they are much thicker than water, we might also think they are heavier. Let's do a test to see.

Equipment Needed

- glass jar with a lid that fits well
- 2 tablespoons of motor oil (used for cars or lawn mowers)
- 2 tablespoons of petroleum jelly
- water
- safety glasses and smock recommended

Activity

1. Fill a glass jar about half full of water.

2. Add the 2 tablespoons of petroleum jelly.

3. Observe, then discard the water and petroleum jelly.

4. Next, refill the glass jar with water (about half full).

5. Add 2 tablespoons of motor oil.

6. Observe.

Additional Notes

✝ **Scripture**
I will exalt you, my God the King; I will praise your name for ever and ever. (Psalm 145:1)

◉ **Discovery Zone**
The word hydrogen *comes from two ancient Greek words: the Greek word* hydro *means water and the Greek word* genes *means creator. So, hydrogen actually means water creator. Do you think that is because water is made from hydrogen plus oxygen?*

7. Tighten the lid securely.

8. Shake the water and oil vigorously and try to get them mixed.

9. Set the jar down and allow the contents to settle for a few moments.

10. Observe.

Think about It

1. What did you observe regarding the petroleum jelly and water? Were you surprised?

   _____

   _____

2. Which was heavier, the water or the motor oil? How do you know?

   _____

   _____

3. Did the water and oil mix? Why do you think they didn't?

   _____

   _____

Lesson 25

Teaching Time:
Attack of the Alkanes

Alkanes, alkenes, and alkynes are the three major types of hydrocarbons made of only hydrogen atoms and carbon atoms. The difference between these three groups is the type of covalent bond between two carbon atoms. For the alkane group, the covalent bonds between the carbon atoms are all single covalent bonds. This means that between each carbon there is only one covalent bond. The propane molecule has a single bond between the three carbons that make up its chain.

➡ **Name It!**
alkane
A type of hydrocarbon with single covalent bonds between the carbon atoms.

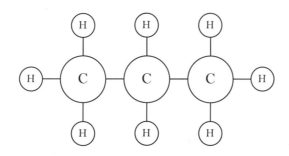

Additional Notes

Each carbon atom is able to have four single bonds. The simplest alkane is methane gas with a molecular formula of CH_4. The next one is the ethane molecule, with two carbons with a single bond between them. The third alkane is propane. Have you noticed that the names of these compounds all end with the suffix *–ane*? That's because they are alkanes. Here is a list of some alkanes:

- methane — CH_4
- ethane — C_2H_6
- propane — C_3H_8
- butane — C_4H_{10}
- pentane — C_5H_{12}
- hexane — C_6H_{14}
- octane — C_8H_{18}

Notice that after the first three, the prefix for the compound is based on the latin word for the number of carbons. *Pent* for five, *hex* for six, *hept* for seven, *oct* for eight. It goes on to even higher numbers. If you saw an alkane with the name of decane, you could look up dec in the latin and find out it means 10 and know that there are 10 carbons in a chain.

Review It

1. For the _____ group, the covalent bonds between the carbon atoms are all single covalent bonds.

2. Alkanes, alkenes, and alkynes are the three major types of hydrocarbons made of only _____ atoms and _____ atoms.

Lesson 25: Alkanes

3. The _____ molecule has a single bond between the two carbons that make up its chain.

4. The alkane compounds have an _____ suffix at the end.

5. A compound with the formula C_4H_{10} is _____.

Hands-On:
Building an Alkane Hydrocarbon Model

What makes alkanes, alkenes, and alkynes different is their chemical structure. This is due to the number of covalent bonds present as well as the number of carbons and hydrogens present. The arrangement, bonding, and number of atoms can make all the difference in something chemically. For example, the salt we use — sodium chloride — is good and healthy for us. However, sodium by itself is an explosive metal. Chlorine by itself is poisonous. However, when bonded together, they become the salt we depend on. For this reason, we will be looking at the structure of the alkanes, alkenes, and alkynes closely in our Hands-On for these three chapters.

Additional Notes

✝ **Scripture**
I will praise the Lord all my life; I will sing praise to my God as long as I live. (Psalm 146:2)

◉ **Discovery Zone**
The element of lead (Pb) is added to ordinary glass to make fine glasses, bowls, and vases. The lead reflects the light and makes the glass appear shinier.

Equipment Needed

- three Styrofoam balls (2-inch diameter)
- eight Styrofoam balls (1-inch diameter)
- 10 round toothpicks

Activity

Using the diagram from the lesson, construct a model of the propane molecule. Feel free to label or paint the carbons and hydrogens differently. If you want to, try to make a methane molecule and an ethane molecule.

Think about It

1. Propane is used as a fuel for heating. Do you know any other uses for propane? (Hint: Do you ever cook outside?)

   _____

   _____

2. Do you think that when propane is burned, it is a solid, liquid, or gas?

   _____

   _____

3. Look at the toothpicks between all the Styrofoam balls. What type of bonds do they represent?

   _____

   _____

Lesson 26

Teaching Time:
Keen on Alkenes

The alkenes are very much like alkanes except they have at least one double bond between carbon atoms. Remember there are four covalent bonding sites on a carbon atom. The double bond means there are four electrons shared in the bond instead of two electrons. Two bonds are better than one and this makes the double bond stronger than the single bond. The simplest alkene is ethene, with a chemical formula of C_2H_4. This means there are two carbon atoms bonded together, using two of each carbon atom's bonding sites, forming a very strong double covalent bond. There are then only four bonding sites left on the two carbons, so only four hydrogens can attach.

→ **Name It!**
Alkene
A type of hydrocarbon with at least one double bond between the carbon atoms.

Additional Notes

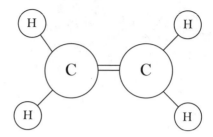

Notice that the picture shows that there are still a total of four bonds around each carbon atom. Can you count them? Make sure you count each line. Propene is the next member of the alkene family with three carbons and six hydrogens. Just like the ethene, propene has two of its carbons bonded with a double co-valent bond, which gives it strength. Alkenes are made from petroleum, just like the alkanes. Here are three alkenes:

- C_2H_4 — ethene
- C_3H_6 — propene
- C_4H_8 — butene

Now see if you can draw the structure of propene. It's a little tricky. It sort of looks like a sheep.

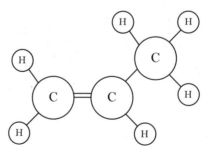

Review It

1. The alkenes are like alkanes except they have at least one

    _____ bond between carbon atoms.

Lesson 26: Alkenes

2. The simplest alkene is _____ with a chemical formula of C_2H_4.

3. The double bond is _____ than the single bond.

4. The formula for propene is _____.

5. There are _____ covalent bonding sites on a carbon atom.

Hands-On:
Building an Alkene Hydrocarbon Model

By now, you should be getting the idea that the differences in alkanes, alkenes, and alkynes is their chemical structure. In the last lesson, we made a model of the propane molecule to help us visualize its composition and bonds. In this Hands-On we are going to build a propene molecule, which has the same number of carbon atoms but only six hydrogens.

Equipment Needed

- three Styrofoam balls (2-inch diameter)
- six Styrofoam balls (1-inch diameter)
- nine round toothpicks

Additional Notes

Scripture
The Lord is gracious and compassionate, slow to anger and rich in love. (Psalm 145:8)

Discovery Zone
Have you ever heard of dry ice? It is actually carbon dioxide (CO_2), which is a gas at room temperature. If it is cooled to $-78°C$, it becomes a solid.

Activity

Using the diagram from the lesson, construct a model of the propene molecule. Once again, feel free to label or paint the carbons and hydrogens differently.

Think about It

1. Describe the differences between the propane and propene molecules in terms of numbers of bonds, hydrogens, and carbons.

   _____

   _____

2. Hold your model and try to pull it apart at a point where there is only a single bond (toothpick). Try to pull it apart where the double bond (two toothpicks) are. Can you feel any difference?

   _____

   _____

3. What kinds of bonds are in this molecule?

   _____

   _____

Lesson 27

Teaching Time:
All Kinds of Alkynes

The alkynes are like the alkanes and the alkenes in that they are made up entirely of carbons and hydrogens. This time, there is at least one triple covalent bond between the carbon atoms. An alkyne uses three of the four covalent bonding sites on a carbon atom just to bond two carbons together. In a triple bond, the two carbon atoms share six electrons. Propyne is an example of an alkyne. The figure that follows illustrates a propyne molecule.

→ **Name It!**
Alkyne
A type of hydrocarbon with at least one triple covalent bond between the carbon atoms.

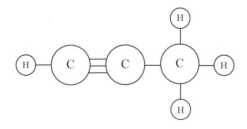

227

Additional Notes

Count the bonds around the carbon atoms. There are still four on each carbon. There are three used for the triple bond and the other one is used for a hydrogen atom. Have you figured out that if the compound has three carbons, it has the prefix *pro-*? The suffix is changed to *–ane* for the single-bonded alkanes, to *–ene* for double-bonded alkenes, and to *–yne* for the triple-bonded alkynes. Look back at the previous lessons to see propane and propene. See if you can redraw the structure of propyne.

Review It

1. The alkynes are like the alkanes and the alkenes in that they are made up entirely of _____ and _____.

2. Alkynes have at least one triple _____ _____ between the carbon atoms.

3. An _____ uses three of the four covalent bonding sites on a carbon atom just to bond two carbons together.

4. The suffix _____ is used in the name of the triple-bonded alkynes.

Lesson 27: Alkynes

5. In alkynes, there are _____ bonds on a carbon used for the triple bond between two carbon atoms, and the other bond site has a hydrogen atom attached.

Hands-On:
Building an Alkyne Hydrocarbon Model

You should have no trouble remembering the differences between the chemical structure of alkanes, alkenes, and alkynes. In this Hands-On we are going to finish our hydrocarbon model collection by building a propyne molecule. Again there will be three carbon atoms, but this time there will be a triple bond between two of the carbons, leaving room for four hydrogens.

Equipment Needed

- three Styrofoam balls (2-inch diameter)
- four Styrofoam balls (1-inch diameter)
- eight round toothpicks

Activity

Using the diagram from the lesson, construct a model of the propyne molecule. As usual, feel free to label or paint the carbons and hydrogens differently.

Additional Notes

✝ **Scripture**
The Lord is good to all; he has compassion on all he has made. (Psalm 145:9)

⊙ **Discovery Zone**
Have you ever heard of a neon sign? The noble gas neon (Ne) isn't reactive, but it can be energized using electricity and it gives off a red-orange color. That is why neon is used to light up signs.

Think about It

1. Describe the differences between the propane, propene, and propyne molecules in terms of numbers of bonds, hydrogen atoms, and carbon atoms.

   _____

   _____

2. Hold your model and try to pull it apart at a point where there is only a single bond (toothpick). Try to pull it apart where the triple bond (three toothpicks) are. Can you feel any difference?

   _____

   _____

3. What kinds of bonds are in this molecule?

   _____

   _____

Lesson 28

ALCoHOLS

Teaching Time:
AlcOHols

There are other organic compounds besides hydrocarbons. Remember, we said that organic chemistry compounds are divided into hydrocarbons and hydrocarbon derivatives. *Derivative* means that the compounds came from something else. So a hydrocarbon derivative comes from a hydrocarbon. We learned a little about hydrocarbons and the three families of alkanes, alkenes, and alkynes. We know that they are made up of only hydrogen and carbon atoms. Now we will talk about hydrocarbon derivatives. They are similar to hydrocarbons but they have additional atoms that make them different. There are many kinds of hydrocarbon derivatives. One is called alcohols.

An **alcohol** is formed when an OH group is substituted for one of the hydrogen atoms on the hydrocarbon. An **OH group** is really just an oxygen atom bonded to a hydrogen, and when an OH group is added to a hydrocarbon, it is called an alcohol. Remember, the simplest hydrocarbon is methane, CH_4. If the OH group is substituted for one of the hydrogen atoms in CH_4,

➲ **Name It!**

<u>alcohol</u>
Formed when an OH group is substituted for one of the hydrogen atoms on the hydrocarbon.

<u>OH group</u>
An oxygen atom bonded to a hydrogen atom.

233

Additional Notes

it is called methanol and its formula is $CH_3\text{-}OH$. Methanol is a liquid and a very deadly poison. It is used to make plastics and antifreeze. Ethanol is another alcohol; its formula is $C_2H_5\text{-}OH$. Ethanol is used to dissolve many compounds and to make other organic compounds. Some people drink ethanol, which is found in beverages such as beer. Technically, ethanol is a poison in any amount and must be detoxified (made into safer compounds) by the human liver in order to remove it from the body. The following figure compares methane to methanol.

Take a close look at these two compounds. Can you see the difference?

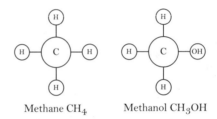

Methane CH_4 Methanol CH_3OH

Review It

1. Organic chemistry compounds are divided into hydrocarbons and hydrocarbon _____.

2. An _____ is formed when an OH group is substituted for one of the hydrogen atoms on the hydrocarbon.

3. In order to make an alcohol, a _____ atom is removed and replaced with an OH group.

Lesson 28: AlcOHols

4. _____ is an alcohol and it has a formula of CH₃-OH.

5. Ethanol is an alcohol with the formula of _____.

Hands-On:
Evaluating the Freezing Point of Alcohol

In lesson 22, we got some experience with freezing point differences between relatively pure water and water with sodium chloride dissolved in it. Remember that individual elements have freezing points (solidification points), melting points, and boiling points. Elements that are combined together into compounds also have freezing points, melting points, and boiling points unique to those compounds. In the Hands-On for lesson 22, we lowered the freezing point of water by dissolving table salt in the water. Now that we've learned about alcohols, let's see if we can change the freezing point of water again — this time by adding some isopropyl alcohol (rubbing alcohol) to the water. In general, alcohol is made of carbon, hydrogen, and oxygen. The chemical formula for isopropyl alcohol is C_3H_8O and it has a freezing point of −128°F. By adding a little alcohol to water, the freezing point of water will be lowered, which means that it won't freeze at 32°F. In fact, it won't freeze at all unless your freezer gets colder than 0°F.

Additional Notes

Equipment Needed

- three clean plastic margarine or butter containers with lids
- isopropyl alcohol or rubbing alcohol (70% solution)
- thermometer that can measure the temperature of the freezer (optional)
- measuring cup
- safety glasses and smock recommended

Activity

Sample	2-Hour Observation	24-Hour Observation	Notes (if any)
Freezer Temperature			
Water Only			
Water and 70% Isopropyl Alcohol			
70% Isopropyl Alcohol			
Other			
Other			
Other			
Other			

Lesson 28: AlcOHols

1. Label one container "Water Only."

2. Label a second container "70% Isopropyl Alcohol."

3. Label a third container "Water and 70% Isopropyl Alcohol."

4. Fill the container labeled "Water Only" with 100 milliliters of water.

5. Fill the container labeled "70% Isopropyl Alcohol" with 100 milliliters of isopropyl alcohol.

6. Fill the container labeled "Water and 70% Isopropyl Alcohol" with 50 milliliters of isopropyl alcohol and 50 milliliters of water.

7. Cover all containers to prevent the alcohol vapors from spreading into the refrigerator compartment.

8. Place all three containers into the freezer.

9. Place the thermometer anywhere inside the freezer.

10. Wait about two hours and check on the cups.

11. Record your observations.

12. Read the temperature of the freezer (optional).

13. In about 24 hours recheck the cups.

14. Record your observations.

🕀 **Scripture**
The Lord is faithful to all his promises and loving toward all he has made. (Psalm 145:13b)

◉ **Discovery Zone**
The five cent coin that we call a nickel is actually only 25% nickel. Most of it is copper.

Think about It

1. Were you able to get any temperature readings from the freezer? What was the reading?

   _____

   _____

2. Do you think the temperatures of the samples were colder than the freezer temperature? Why or why not?

   _____

   _____

3. Do you think if less alcohol were used in the water that the sample would freeze? Test it out by using less and less alcohol.

   _____

   _____

4. Record your observations in the spaces labeled "Other" on the chart.

Lesson 29

Teaching time:
Ester (As in Polyester)

Esters are pretty amazing. We are going to examine some of these, but first let's figure out what the esters are and what they look like chemically. Remember, besides the hydrocarbons, there are also the hydrocarbon derivatives. In the last lesson, we studied one of these derivatives — alcohols. Well, esters are another hydrocarbon derivative.

Esters are formed by a chemical reaction of alcohols and acids. In the reaction, a carbon-based molecule is formed that is bonded to a hydrocarbon chain. Depending on which acid and alcohol are used in the reaction, a variety of esters can be made, but they all have one thing in common — the presence of the ester group, which looks like this:

○ **Name It!**
<u>esters</u>
Formed by a chemical reaction of alcohols and acids.

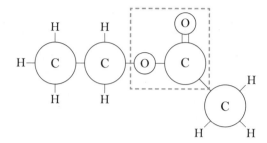

The ester group is surrounded by a dotted line. This is the molecular structure of an ester called ethyl ethanoate (sometimes called ethyl acetate) — the solvent used in fingernail polish.

Esters are found naturally in many plants. They are the chemical compound in flowers that makes the fragrance of the flower. Esters are also found in fruits; they produce the flavor of the fruit. When artificial flavors are made in a lab, they are esters. There is a pretty complicated reaction required to make a very large ester that we know as polyester. That's right, there is an ester called poly ethylene glycol terephthalate, which is used to make clothes and other textile items. Take a look at some of the tags on your clothing and see if you see the word polyester.

Review It

1. Esters are another hydrocarbon _____.

2. Esters are formed by a reaction of _____ and _____.

3. Depending on the acid and alcohol used in the reaction, a variety of _____ can be made.

4. Esters are found naturally in many _____.

Lesson 29: Esters

5. Esters are recognizable because of the presence of the _____.

Hands-On:
The Crayon as a Hydrocarbon Product

In this unit, we have been looking at a variety of hydrocarbons, alcohols, and, finally in this last lesson, esters. There is a product that we are all very familiar with that actually is made of the things we have been studying. Believe it or not, it is the crayon. Crayons are made of hydrocarbons, alcohols, esters, and fatty acids. So, as a treat, we are going to do some serious coloring for this Hands-On. We have a coloring page for this.

Equipment Needed

- crayons

Activity

1. Enjoy the coloring page.

The coloring page section is located on pages 269 – 279.

✝ **Scripture**
The Lord watches over all who love him. (Psalm 145:20a)

◉ **Discovery Zone**
When worn by a person, perfumes and colognes are heated up by the skin, making the molecules move faster and go into the air. This is how we are able to smell the different scents.

Think about It

1. As you were coloring, did you think about the various compounds that are combined together to form the crayon?

   _____

   _____

2. Crayons are solids. Do you think at some time they were liquid in order to form them into their shapes?

   _____

   _____

3. Can you remember what compounds were used to make the crayons?

   _____

   _____

Lesson 30
BIOCHEMISTRY

Teaching Time:
Biological Chemistry

The area of organic chemistry called biochemistry is exactly what the name implies. It is the study of the chemical processes of biology. More specifically, **biochemistry** examines the chemistry of living things. The composition of living things and the chemicals that make them function are largely organic compounds and molecules. Among these compounds and molecules are four important groups called macromolecules, which means *big* molecules. Those macromolecules are proteins, carbohydrates, fats, and nucleic acids, and they are considered to be the building blocks of all life. Living things can make these macromolecules for use in living processes. Sometimes one organism eats another organism (like people eating fish or chicken), and then these macromolecules are available to be used in living processes as well. The field of biochemistry is an advanced topic because the chemical mechanisms for making or using these macromolecules is complex. We will examine some of the important features of the four

➜ **Name It!**
<u>biochemistry</u>
The study of the chemistry of living things.

Additional Notes

macromolecules and hopefully help you understand that only God could have made every living thing and provided them with everything they need to live.

Nucleic Acids

Nucleic acids are information molecules. Deoxyribonucleic acid (DNA) and ribonucleic acid (RNA) are the names of the nucleic acids found in both plants and animals. Chromosomes, containing genes, are composed mainly of DNA. DNA and RNA contain the code that is able to direct the order in which amino acids go together. Amino acids are building-block molecules that make up proteins. The DNA is an extremely large molecule made up of other molecules. The DNA molecule is coiled up as a chromosome, but if it were uncoiled and measured end to end it could be several feet long.

Proteins

There are many types of proteins that are at work in living things. Different proteins make up most of the structure of cells, muscle tissue, skin, hormones, antibodies, enzymes, and so forth. Depending on the order that the amino acids are in, different proteins have different purposes. Living organisms make the proteins they need — that goes for us humans as well. To make a protein, an organism needs to get amino acids from somewhere. When certain foods containing protein are consumed (like meat, eggs, and beans), the protein is broken up into amino acids and then the amino acids are reassembled to make new proteins.

Carbohydrates

Carbohydrates are another important group of macromolecules. Carbohydrates, which include sugars, starches, and fiber, are used for energy in plants and animals. A carbohydrate is a

Lesson 30: Biochemistry

large molecule made of smaller molecules that are covalently bonded to each other. The large carbohydrate molecule is called polysaccharide, and the small molecules that make up the carbohydrate are called monosaccharides. **Monosaccharides** are sugars (such as glucose and fructose), which are made of carbon, oxygen, and hydrogen. In the human body, these monosaccharides are used as fuel; in other words, they are a source of energy.

A **polysaccharide** is a polymer that is made of many monosaccharides bonded together. Starch is a polysaccharide made up of many glucose molecules bonded together. The glucose molecules are arranged in a long, straight-chain with a few side chains of glucose molecules. A starch polysaccharide can have between 3,000 and 18,000 glucose molecules. You can see that starch will provide a lot of energy for a person who eats starch. Starch is found in vegetables, such as potatoes and corn, and in grains, such as wheat and rice.

Fats

Some fat is important for living things because it is used in bodily processes to produce other necessary substances for life. We can get fat from many of the foods we eat, such as butter or meat. When we consume more food than we need for energy, the extra can be converted to fat and stored in fat cells. Those cells allow animals to store energy for later use. Fat can release a large amount of energy, if needed.

Review It

1. Nucleic acids are _____ molecules:

   deoxyribonucleic acid (DNA) and ribonucleic acid (RNA).

> **Name It!**
> **monosaccharides**
> *Sugars (such as glucose and fructose), which are made of carbon, oxygen, and hydrogen.*
>
> **polysaccharide**
> *A polymer that is made of many monosaccharides bonded together.*

Additional Notes

2. Depending on the sequence of _____ _____, different proteins are made for different purposes.

3. The large _____ molecule is called polysaccharide.

4. Monosaccharides are sugars such as _____ and _____.

5. Fat cells allow animals to store _____ for later use.

Hands-On:
Evaluating Products for Macromolecules

You might be surprised to discover what the protein, carbohydrate, and fat composition of our food is. Having a high or low content of one of these macromolecules doesn't necessarily make the food good or bad. However, from a chemistry perspective, it is interesting. In this Hands-On, we are going to examine some different foods and compare the nutritional facts about each one in a chart. You can probably find some of these foods in your kitchen, or you can go shopping and take some notes at the store.

Lesson 30: Biochemistry

Equipment Needed

- pencil

Activity

Product	Protein	Carbohydrates	Fat	Serving Size
Perrier water				
Coke				
Pepsi				
Grits	3 grams	29 grams	0.5 grams	1/4 cup
Wheaties cereal				
Kelloggs Special K cereal				
Minute Maid orange juice				
Minute Maid Lemonade				
M&M's Chocolate Candies				
M&M's Peanut Chocolate Candies				

1. Look at the example on the chart.

2. Find each of the products listed on the chart.

Additional Notes

Scripture
I praise you because I am fearfully and wonderfully made; your works are wonderful, I know that full well. (Psalm 139: 14)

Discovery Zone
Have you ever had poison ivy? The itchy rash is caused by a chemical called urushiol, which is in the poison ivy plant. When you touch the plant, the urushiol gets on your skin and causes the rash.

3. Examine the nutritional information (included on a label on each product).

4. Complete the chart for each of the three macromolecules that may be in a serving of the product.

Think about It

1. What product had the most carbohydrate content?

   _____

   _____

2. Was there a difference between Coke and Pepsi?

   _____

   _____

3. What differences did you note between the two types of M&M's candies? Can you explain the differences?

   _____

   _____

4. Compare the two Minute Maid juices.

   _____

   _____

Lesson 30: Biochemistry

5. Compare the two cereals.

_____

_____

Unit Five Wrap-Up
Show What You Know!

Study Notes

1. _____ are a family of compounds that are made of various combinations and amounts of the element hydrogen and the element carbon.
    a. Hydrocarbons
    b. Hydroxyl groups
    c. Cheeseburgers

2. Hydrocarbons make up a type of chemistry called _____.
    a. hydrogen chemistry
    b. organic chemistry
    c. complicated chemistry

3. The simplest hydrocarbon compound is _____ gas with the formula of CH_4.
    a. mostly
    b. methane
    c. propane

4. Carbon atoms have _____ available bonding sites.
    a. no
    b. 2
    c. 4

Study Notes

5. For the _____ group, the covalent bonds between the carbon atoms are all single covalent bonds.
    a. alkyne
    b. alkane
    c. al capone

6. Alkanes, alkenes, and alkynes are the three major types of hydrocarbons made of only _____ atoms and _____ atoms.
    a. carbon, hydrogen
    b. carbon, oxygen
    c. big, little

7. The alkane compounds have an _____ suffix at the end.
    a. -yne
    b. -ing
    c. -ane

8. The alkenes are like alkanes except they have at least one _____ bond between carbon atoms.
    a. double
    b. triple
    c. superglue

9. The simplest alkene is _____ with a chemical formula of C_2H_4.
    a. ethene
    b. propene
    c. hot chocolate

Unit Five Wrap-Up

10. The alkynes are like the alkanes and the alkenes in that they are made up entirely of _____ and _____.
    a. carbon, hydrogen
    b. carbon, sodium
    c. chocolate, vanilla

11. _____ use three of the four covalent bonding sites on a carbon atom just to bond two carbons together.
    a. Alkynes
    b. Alkanes
    c. Tuna salads

12. The suffix _____ is used in the name of the triple-bonded alkynes.
    a. -yne
    b. -ene
    c. -ing

13. Organic chemistry compounds are divided into hydrocarbons and hydrocarbon _____.
    a. derivatives
    b. lunches
    c. molecules

14. _____ are formed when an OH group is substituted for one of the hydrogen atoms on the hydrocarbon.
    a. Esters
    b. Alcohols
    c. Giant cats

Study Notes

Study Notes

15. Esters are another hydrocarbon _____.
    a. problem
    b. derivative
    c. particle

16. Esters are formed by a reaction of _____ and _____.
    a. acids, alcohols
    b. acids, bases
    c. mustard, pickles

17. Depending on the _____ and _____ used in the reaction, a variety of esters can be made.
    a. time, temperature
    b. acid, base
    c. acid, alcohol

18. Esters are found naturally in many _____.
    a. plants
    b. starships
    c. bacteria

19. Esters are recognizable because of the presence of the _____.
    a. free food
    b. ester group
    c. chemical reaction

20. More bonds between carbon atoms mean more _____.
    a. fun
    b. strength
    c. carbons

Unit Five Wrap-Up

21. Nucleic acids are _____ molecules.
    a. inorganic
    b. mixed up
    c. information

22. Depending on the sequence of _____, different proteins are made for different purposes.
    a. silverware
    b. amino acids
    c. carbohydrate molecules

23. The large _____ molecule is called polysaccharide.
    a. hydrogen
    b. carbohydrate
    c. candy bar

24. Monosaccharides are sugars such as _____ and _____
    a. glucose, fructose
    b. garden hose, radiator hose
    c. fat, protein

25. Fat cells allow animals to store _____ for later use.
    a. heat
    b. energy
    c. sun tan lotion

Study Notes

Glossary

acid — a chemical compound that donates or gives away a proton (called a hydrogen ion) in a reaction.

alcohol — formed when an OH group is substituted for one of the hydrogen atoms on the hydrocarbon.

alkane — a type of hydrocarbon with single covalent bonds between the carbon atoms.

alkene — a type of hydrocarbon with at least one double bond between the carbon atoms.

alkyne — a type of hydrocarbon with at least one triple covalent bond between the carbon atoms.

apparatus — the equipment that a chemist uses, including containers, funnels, and tubing.

atom — the smallest part of an element that can exist alone. All matter is made up of atoms.

Additional Notes

atomic number — each element has an atomic number. It is equal to the number of protons in one atom of the element.

bases — a chemical compound that accepts or receives a proton (called a hydrogen ion) in a reaction.

binary — two.

binary compound — a compound that contains two different elements.

biochemistry — the study of the matter of living things.

biology — the study of living things.

boiling point — the temperature at which a liquid becomes a gas.

carbon — the main ingredient in the fuels and oil used in our cars and aircraft. It is also part of the clothes we wear and the food we eat. It is one of the main ingredients for life itself and an essential ingredient for parts of our bodies and how we function.

chemical bond — a very strong force between atoms that holds them together.

chemical formula — a formula that tells us what a compound is made of – the kinds and amounts of each element.

chemical name — the name given to a compound based on specific rules.

chemical nomenclature — the system of rules and procedures for naming chemical compounds.

chemical properties — the ways matter reacts with other types of matter in a chemical reaction.

Glossary

chemical reaction — the actual event when chemicals come together and bond.

chemist — a specially trained scientist who studies and works with matter.

chemistry — the structured and formal study of matter, how it can change, and how it reacts with other matter.

compound — a substance that is made up of two or more elements.

covalent bond — a bond that occurs between two atoms when these atoms share electrons.

dilute solution — a solution in which just a small amount of a solute is dissolved.

electron — the only type of particle found in the extranuclear region of an atom; it has a negative electrical charge.

element — the purest form of matter that exists.

energy — light, electricity, and heat. Energy is used and produced in chemical reactions.

equation — the expression in writing of a chemical reaction.

esters — formed by a chemical reaction of alcohols and acids.

extranuclear region — the area outside the nucleus, but still part of the atom.

freezing point — the temperature at which a liquid freezes.

Additional Notes

Additional Notes

gas — a state of matter in which the substance is airlike and does not have a definite shape or a definite volume.

hydrocarbons — a family of compounds that are made of various combinations and amounts of the element hydrogen and the element carbon.

ionic bond — a bond that occurs when one or more electrons from one atom is transferred to another atom.

ions — atoms with extra electrons or those missing electrons.

inorganic chemistry — the study of matter that does not contain any carbon.

interpolate — to estimate a measurement.

isotope — an atom that has gained neutrons.

lab coat — a smock or shirt that protects a chemist's clothing from chemicals and even water. It also has some pockets to hold a pencil and safety glasses.

liquid — a state of matter in which the substance flows (like water), has a constant volume, and takes on the shape of its container.

matter — anything that takes up or occupies space.

melting point — the temperature at which a solid melts.

mixtures — made of two or more pure substances or compounds that are physically combined (mixed) together but not chemically bonded.

molecule — two or more atoms joined together.

Glossary

monosaccharides — sugars (such as glucose and fructose), which are made of carbon, oxygen, and hydrogen.

neutron — a type of particle found in the nucleus of an atom; it has a neutral electrical charge.

nucleus — the center of the atom.

OH group — an oxygen atom bonded to a hydrogen atoms.

organic chemistry — the study of matter that contains a substance called carbon; the study of hydrocarbons.

organic compounds — carbon compounds.

periodic law of chemistry — states that when the elements are arranged in a table according to their atomic number, elements with similar properties occur at regular intervals called periods.

periodic table of the elements — sometimes called the periodic chart; this table is a list of elements arranged according to the element's atomic number.

physical properties — characteristics of matter, such as color, odor, taste, boiling point, and melting point.

physics — the scientific study of both matter and energy in great detail.

polysaccharide — a polymer that is made of many monosaccharides bonded together.

products — what remains after a chemical reaction takes place.

proton — a type of particle found in the nucleus of an atom; it has a positive electrical charge.

Additional Notes

Additional Notes

reactants — the substances we begin with in a chemical reaction.

safety glasses — glasses that protect a chemist's eyes during experiments.

salt — one of the products of a reaction between an acid and a base.

saturated solution — a solution of the greatest amount of solute that can be dissolved into a solvent at a given temperature.

solid — any kind of matter that has a definite shape.

solute — the substance present in a solution in a lesser amount.

solution — two or more substances (either a compound or an element) mixed very well together so that all the different atoms and molecules are evenly distributed.

solvent — the substance present in a solution in the greatest amount.

state change — when matter changes from one state to another.

states — all matter can exist in three different states: solid, liquid, or gas

COLORING PAGES

Chemistry is often studied in a lab. However, chemistry is an explanation of the way God has wonderfully put together the matter of the universe. When we see the things that make up the earth, both living things and non-living things, we can appreciate the chemistry that describes God's creation. These coloring pages remind us that the atoms, molecules, and compounds of chemistry make up all things, including the stars above, the places where we live, the food we eat, and all living things.

The following coloring pages provide examples of the diversity and significance of chemistry in our lives, the world, and the universe.

© 2005 by Bright Ideas Press

For use after Unit One Wrap-Up

For Use with Lesson 29 Hands-On

appendix A

ELEMENT TABLES

See pages 282 – 283 for the List of Elements and Their Symbols.
See page 284 for the Periodic Table of Elements.

Additional Notes

List of Elements and Their Symbols

Element	Symbol	Element	Symbol
Actinium	Ac	Fluorine	F
Aluminum	Al	Francium	Fr
Americium	Am	Gadolinium	Gd
Antimony	Sb	Gallium	Ga
Argon	Ar	Germanium	Ge
Arsenic	As	Gold	Au
Astatine	At	Hafnium	Hf
Barium	Ba	Hassium	Hs
Berkelium	Bk	Helium	He
Beryllium	Be	Holmium	Ho
Bismuth	Bi	Hydrogen	H
Bohrium	Bh	Indium	In
Boron	B	Iodine	I
Bromine	Br	Iridium	Ir
Cadmium	Cd	Iron	Fe
Calcium	Ca	Krypton	Kr
Californium	Cf	Lanthanum	La
Carbon	C	Lawrencium	Lr
Cerium	Ce	Lead	Pb
Cesium	Cs	Lithium	Li
Chlorine	Cl	Lutetium	Lu
Chromium	Cr	Magnesium	Mg
Cobalt	Co	Manganese	Mn
Copper	Cu	Meitnerium	Mt
Curium	Cm	Mendelevium	Md
Darmstadtium	Ds	Mercury	Hg
Dubnium	Db	Molybdenum	Mo
Dysprosium	Dy	Neodymium	Nd
Einsteinium	Es	Neon	Ne
Erbium	Er	Neptunium	Np
Europium	Eu	Nickel	Ni
Fermium	Fm	Niobium	Nb

Appendix A: Element Tables

Element	Symbol	Element	Symbol
Nitrogen	N	Strontium	Sr
Nobelium	No	Sulfur	S
Osmium	Os	Tantalum	Ta
Oxygen	O	Technetium	Tc
Palladium	Pd	Tellurium	Te
Phosphorus	P	Terbium	Tb
Platinum	Pt	Thallium	Tl
Plutonium	Pu	Thorium	Th
Polonium	Po	Thulium	Tm
Potassium	K	Tin	Sn
Praseodymium	Pr	Titanium	Ti
Promethium	Pm	Tungsten	W
Protactinium	Pa	Ununbium	Uub
Radium	Ra	Ununhexium	Uuh
Radon	Rn	Ununium	Uuu
Rhenium	Re	Ununoctium	Uuo
Rhodium	Rh	Ununpentium	Uup
Rubidium	Rb	Ununquadium	Uuq
Ruthenium	Ru	Ununseptium	Uus
Rutherfordium	Rf	Ununtrium	Uut
Samarium	Sm	Uranium	U
Scandium	Sc	Vanadium	V
Seaborgium	Sg	Xenon	Xe
Selenium	Se	Ytterbium	Yb
Silicon	Si	Yttrium	Y
Silver	Ag	Zinc	Zn
Sodium	Na	Zirconium	Zr

Additional Notes

Periodic Table of the Elements

☐ Non-metal
☐ Metal

	Group IA	Group IIA	Group IIIB	Group IVB	Group VB	Group VIB	Group VIIB	Group VIIIB			Group IB	Group IIB	Group IIIA	Group IVA	Group VA	Group VIA	Group VIIA	Group VIIIA
Period 1	H 1 1.01																	He 2 4.00
Period 2	Li 3 6.94	Be 4 9.01											B 5 10.81	C 6 12.01	N 7 14.01	O 8 16.00	F 9 19.00	Ne 10 20.18
Period 3	Na 11 22.79	Mg 12 24.31											Al 13 26.98	Si 14 28.09	P 15 30.97	S 16 32.06	Cl 17 35.45	Ar 18 39.95
Period 4	K 19 39.10	Ca 20 40.08	Sc 21 44.96	Ti 22 47.90	V 23 50.94	Cr 24 52.00	Mn 25 54.94	Fe 26 55.85	Co 27 58.93	Ni 28 58.70	Cu 29 63.55	Zn 30 65.38	Ga 31 69.72	Ge 32 72.59	As 33 74.92	Se 34 78.96	Br 35 79.90	Kr 36 83.80
Period 5	Rb 37 85.47	Sr 38 87.62	Y 39 88.91	Zr 40 91.22	Nb 41 92.91	Mo 42 95.94	Tc 43 98	Ru 44 101.07	Rh 45 102.91	Pd 46 106.4	Ag 47 107.87	Cd 48 112.40	In 49 114.82	Sn 50 118.69	Sb 51 121.75	Te 52 127.60	I 53 126.90	Xe 54 131.30
Period 6	Cs 55 132.91	Ba 56 137.33	La 57 138.91	Hf 72 178.49	Ta 73 180.95	W 74 183.85	Re 75 186.21	Os 76 190.2	Ir 77 192.22	Pt 78 195.09	Au 79 196.97	Hg 80 200.59	Tl 81 204.37	Pb 82 207.2	Bi 83 208.98	Po 84 209	At 85 210	Rn 86 222
Period 7	Fr 87 223	Ra 88 26.02	Ac 89 227.02															

Ce 58 140.12	Pr 59 140.91	Nd 60 144.24	Pm 61 145	Sm 62 150.4	Eu 63 151.96	Gd 64 157.25	Tb 65 158.93	Dy 66 162.50	Ho 67 164.93	Er 68 167.26	Tm 69 168.93	Yb 70 173.04	Lu 71 174.97
Th 90 232.04	Pa 91 231.04	U 92 238.03	Np 93 237.05	Pu 94 244	Am 95 243	Cm 96 247	Bk 97 247	Cf 98 251	Es 99 252	Fm 100 257	Md 101 258	No 102 259	Lr 103 260

appendix B
RESOURCE LIST
by Rebecca Delvaux

The majority of books in this appendix are likely to be stocked in most public libraries or available through interlibrary loan. Many are also available for purchase from major bookstores or homeschool book retailers. Please use your discretion as you investigate these resources. Many address topics such as evolution, include illustrations that you may deem inappropriate, and may interject thoughts contrary to biblical thought. We have included such resources because there is a glaring lack of explicitly Christian resources on the chemistry topics covered in this book.

Please note the list of chemistry reference books. These may be utilized with every lesson in addition to the other library books, but they are especially helpful for the lessons that have no library books listed. These reference books have illustrations, charts, and explanations that complement *Christian Kids Explore Chemistry* and may be particularly appreciated by younger learners and visual learners of all ages. Note that they are *not* from an explicitly Christian perspective.

I have noted if a resource is appropriate for a particular age group. Unless noted otherwise, books with 32 pages or less are

Additional Notes

lower grammar (LG) books and those with 64 or more pages are upper grammar books (UG). I have also noted if the resource provides adult-level, in-depth topic coverage. Of course, resources of any length may be useful for both lower and upper grammar level children.

Many helpful videos and DVDs are also available to enhance your study of chemistry. A comprehensive list of supplemental videos is available online at www.brightideaspress.com — complete with links to online retailers to simplify your research and shopping. There you will also find lists of games, websites, and magazines to supplement your study of chemistry.

It is my heartfelt prayer that you and your children will be richly blessed by this curriculum and the supplemental resources.

Chemistry Reference Books

A Guide to the Elements by Alvert Stwertka (Oxford University Press; ISBN: 0195150279; 2002; 248pp) FYI: Written for 9 – 12 year olds

Chemistry (Eyewitness Science) by Ann Newmark (Dorling Kindersley; ISBN: 0789448815; 1999; 64pp)

Matter (Eyewitness Science) by Christopher Cooper (Dorling Kindersley; ISBN: 0789448866; 1999; 64pp)

Ultimate Visual Dictionary of Science (Usborne Books; ISBN: 0789435128; 1998; 448pp)

Usborne Illustrated Dictionary of Chemistry (Usborne Books; ISBN: 0746037945; 2000; 128pp)

Usborne Illustrated Dictionary of Science (Usborne Books; ISBN: 0794500641; 2001; 382pp)

Usborne Book of Science (Usborne Books; ISBN: 0746008309; 144pp) Covers chemistry, physics, and biology.

Online chemistry encyclopedia at Science Daily (online magazine); brief listings with illustrations at: www.sciencedaily.com/encyclopedia/chemistry/

Unit One: The Basics of Chemistry

Lesson 1: Introduction to Chemistry?
chemistry reference books

Lesson 2: Chemistry Tools
chemistry reference books

Test Tubes and Beakers: Chemistry for Young Experimenters by E.H. Coulson, A.E.J. Trinder, and Aaron Klein (Doubleday; 1971; 134pp)

Lesson 3: Matter
chemistry reference books

Matter Really Matters (Let's Wonder about Science series) by J.M. Patten (Rourke, ISBN: 1559161248; 1995; 24pp)

Matter (Eyewitness Science) by Chris Cooper (Dorling Kindersley; ISBN: 1879431882; 1992; 64pp)

Lesson 4: Elements
chemistry reference books

The Periodic Kingdom: A Journey into the Land of the Chemical Elements (Science Masters series) by P.W. Atkins (Basic Books; ISBN: 0465072666; 1997; 176pp) Adult

Additional Notes

Additional Notes

Elements, Compounds, and Mixtures (Let's Wonder about Science series) by J.M. Patten (Rourke; ISBN: 1559161272; 1995; 24pp)

What Is the World Made Of? All About Solids, Liquids, and Gases (Let's-Read-and-Find-Out Science Book) by Kathleen Weidner Zoehfeld (HarperCollins; ISBN: 0060271442; 1998; 32pp)

A Guide to the Elements by Albert Stwertka (Oxford University Press; ISBN: 0195150279; 2002; 248pp) FYI: Written for 9–12 year olds

Sparks of Life series by Jean F. Blashfield (Raintree Steck-Vaughn; 2002; 64pp)

- *Magnesium* (ISBN: 0739843605)
- *Iron and the Trace Elements* (ISBN: 0739843591)
- *Chlorine* (ISBN: 0739843583)
- *Sulfur* (ISBN: 0739834525)
- *Potassium* (ISBN: 0739834517)
- *Phosphorus* (ISBN: 0739834509)
- *Sodium* (ISBN: 0817250425)
- *Oxygen* (ISBN: 0817250379) [+Unit 7]
- *Nitrogen* (ISBN: 0817250395)
- *Hydrogen* (ISBN: 0817250387)
- *Carbon* (ISBN: 0817250417) [+Unit 5]
- *Calcium* (ISBN: 0817250409)

The Elements series by Jens Thomas (Benchmark Books; 2002; 32pp)

- *Silicon* (ISBN: 0761412743)
- *Carbon* (ISBN: 0761408789) [+Unit 5]
- *Noble Gases* (ISBN: 0761414622) [+Unit 4]

Appendix B: Resource List

Chemicals in Action series by Chris Oxlade (Heinemann Library; 2002; 48pp)

- *Metals* (ISBN: 1403425000)
- *Elements and Compounds* (ISBN: 1588101967)
- *Atoms* (ISBN: 1588101959)
- *Materials, Changes and Reactions* (ISBN: 1588101975) [+Unit 3]
- *States of Matter* (ISBN: 1588101991) [+Unit 4]

First Books — Chemical Elements series by Karen Fitzgerald (Franklin Watts; 1997; 64pp)

- *The Chemical Elements* (ISBN: 0531194558)
- *The Story of Oxygen* (ISBN: 0531202259)
- *The Story of Nitrogen* (ISBN: 0531202488)
- *The Story of Iron* (ISBN: 0531202704)

Lesson 5: Mixtures and Compounds
chemistry reference books

Unit Two: Atoms and Molecules

Lesson 6: the Atoms
chemistry reference books

Atoms and Molecules (Usborne Understanding Science) by P. Roxbee-Cox and M. Parsonage. (Usborne; ISBN: 1881105899; 32pp) UG+

Lesson 7: Atomic Number
chemistry reference books

Atoms and Molecules (Usborne Understanding Science) by P.

Additional Notes

Additional Notes

Roxbee-Cox and M. Parsonage. (Usborne; ISBN: 1881105899; 32pp) UG+

Lesson 8: Atomic Mass
chemistry reference books

Atoms and Molecules (Usborne Understanding Science) by P. Roxbee-Cox and M. Parsonage. (Usborne; ISBN: 1881105899; 32pp) UG+

Lesson 9: Periodic Table
chemistry reference books

Atoms and Molecules (Usborne Understanding Science) by P. Roxbee-Cox and M. Parsonage (Usborne; ISBN: 1881105899; 32pp) UG+

Lesson 10: Molecules
chemistry reference books

Atoms and Molecules (Usborne Understanding Science) by P. Roxbee-Cox and M. Parsonage. (Usborne; ISBN: 1881105899; 32pp) UG+

The Atoms Family (Let's Wonder about Science series) by J.M. Patten (Rourke; ISBN: 1559161256; 1995; 24pp)

The World of Atoms and Quarks by Albert Stwertka (Twenty-First Century Books; ISBN: 0805035338; 1995; 96pp)

Atoms (Chemicals in Action) by Chris Oxlade (Heinemann Library; ISBN: 1588101959; 48pp)

The Periodic Table (True Book: Elements) by Tocci Salvatore (Children's Press; 2004; 48pp)

Appendix B: Resource List

Adventures With Atoms and Molecules — Chemistry Experiments for Young People, Books I – V (Enslow Publishers; 1998; 82pp)

- Book I (ISBN: 07660122247)
- Book II (ISBN: 076612255)
- Book III (ISBN: 0766012263)
- Book IV (ISBN: 0766012271)
- Book V (ISBN 076601228X)

The Periodic Kingdom: A Journey into the Land of the Chemical Elements (Science Masters Series) by P. W. Atkins (Basic Books; ISBN: 0465072666; 1997; 176pp). An entertaining way to educate yourself about the Periodic Table. Award-winning book written like a travel guide to the "Periodic Kingdom." Adult

Unit 3: The Nature of Chemistry

Lesson 11: Chemical Bonds
chemistry reference books

Lesson 12: More Chemical Bonds
chemistry reference books

Lesson 13: Formulas
chemistry reference books

Lesson 14: Naming Compounds
chemistry reference books

Mixtures and Compounds (Usborne Internet-Linked Library of Science) by A. Smith and P. Clarke (Usborne; ISBN: 1580863779; 64pp) UG

Additional Notes

Additional Notes

Lesson 15: Reactions
chemistry reference books

Chemicals and Reactions by Jon Richards (Copper Beech Books; ISBN: 0761311602; 2002; 32pp)

Chemistry (Eyewitness Science) by Ann Newmark (Dorling Kindersley; ISBN: 0789448815; 1999; 64pp)

Lesson 16: Acids
chemistry reference books

Lesson 17: Bases
chemistry reference books

Acids and Bases by Chris Oxlade (Heinemann Library; ISBN: 1588101940; 2002; 42pp)

Acids and Bases by J.M. Patten (Rourke Book Co.; ISBN: 1559161280; 1995; 24pp)

Lesson 18: Salts
chemistry reference books

Unit 4: States of Matter

Lesson 19: Solids and Liquids
chemistry reference books

Materials (Usborne Internet-Linked Library of Science) by A. Smith (Usborne; ISBN: 1580863787; 64pp) UG

Lesson 20: Gases
chemistry reference books

Appendix B: Resource List

Materials (Usborne Internet-Linked Library of Science) by A. Smith (Usborne, ISBN: 1580863787; 64pp) UG

See biography section

Lesson 21: Gas Laws
chemistry reference books

What Is the World Made Of? All About Solids, Liquids, and Gases by Kathleen Weidner (HarperCollins Publishers; ISBN: 0060271442; 1998; 32pp)

Solids, Liquids, and Gases (Let's Wonder about Science) by J.M. Patten (Rourke; 1995, ISBN: 1559161264; 24pp)

Solid, Liquid, Gas (Rookie Read-About Science) by Fay Robinson (Children's Press; ISBN: 0516460412; 1996; 32pp)

Lesson 22: State Change
chemistry reference books

Liquid to Gas and Back (Let's Wonder about Science series) by J.M. Patten (Rourke; ISBN: 1559161299; 1995; 24pp)

States of Matter (Chemicals in Action series) by Chris Oxlade (Heinemann Library; ISBN: 1588101991; 2002; 48pp)

Materials, Changes and Reactions (Chemicals in Action series) by Chris Oxlade. (Heinemann Library; ISBN: 1588101975; 2002; 48pp)

Lesson 23: Solutions
chemistry reference books

Additional Notes

Additional Notes

Unit 5: Organic Chemistry

Lesson 24: Hydrocarbons
chemistry reference books

Carbon (Sparks of Life series) by Jean F. Blashfield (Raintree Steck-Vaughn; ISBN: 0817250417; 1999; 64pp)

Carbon (The Elements series) by Giles Sparrow (Benchmark Books; ISBN: 0761408789; 1999; 32pp)

Lesson 25: Alkanes
chemistry reference books

Lesson 26: Alkenes
chemistry reference books

Lesson 27: Alkynes
chemistry reference books

Lesson 28: Alcohols
chemistry reference books

Lesson 29: Esters
chemistry reference books

Lesson 30: Biochemistry
chemistry reference books

Human Body (Usborne Internet-Linked Library of Science) by K. Rogers (Usborne; ISBN: 1580863752; 64pp) UG

Darwin's Black Box: The Biochemical Challenge to Evolution by Dr. Michael Behe (Free Press; 0684834936; 1998; 320pp) FYI: Technical biochemistry resource; Adult

Fat Chance: The Chemistry of Lipids (Science in Our World series) edited by Mickey Sarquis (Terrific Science Press; ISBN: 1883822092; 1995; 96pp) FYI: Grades 4 – 12

Additional Chemistry Books

ABC's of Chemistry (Hands on Science series) by Michael Morgolin (J. Weston Walch; ISBN: 0825139317; 2000; 94pp) UG

Chemical Chaos (Horrible Science) by Nick Arnold (Scholastic; ISBN: 0590108859; 1998) UG

Crime Lab Chemistry: A Chromatography Mystery by Jacqueline Barber and Kevin Beals (Consortium; ISBN: 0924886900; 2004; 72pp) UG

Career Ideas for Kids That Like Science by Diane Lindsey Reeves (Facts On File; ISBN: 0816036861; 1998; 176pp)

Exploring the World of Chemistry by John Hudson Tiner (Answers in Genesis; 800-778-3390; www.answersingenesis.org ; 42pp) FYI: Free lesson plans are available online.

From Start to Finish series (Lerner Publishing Group; 2003 and 2004) can be used to launch discussions of how chemistry is involved in all areas of life; LG

- *From Cane to Sugar* (ISBN: 0822509407)
- *From Cement to Bridge* (ISBN: 0822513897)
- *From Clay to Bricks* (ISBN: 0822546639)
- *From Cloth to American Flag* (ISBN: 0822513862)
- *From Cocoa Bean to Chocolate* (ISBN: 0822546655)
- *From Cotton to T-Shirt* (ISBN: 0822546612)
- *From Egg to Butterfly* (ISBN: 0822507137)
- *From Egg to Chicken* (ISBN: 0822546620)

Additional Notes

Additional Notes

- *From Flower to Honey* (ISBN: 082250717X)
- *From Foal to Horse* (ISBN: 0822509415)
- *From Fruit to Jelly* (ISBN: 0822509423)
- *From Grass to Milk* (ISBN: 0822546647)
- *From Idea to Book* (ISBN: 0822513854)
- *From Iron to Car* (ISBN: 0822509431)
- *From Kernel to Corn* (ISBN: 0822546590)
- *From Maple Tree to Syrup* (ISBN: 0822513900)
- *From Metal to Airplane* (ISBN: 0822513889)
- *From Milk to Cheese* (ISBN: 0822513870)
- *From Milk to Ice Cream* (ISBN: 0822507145)
- *From Oil to Gas* (ISBN: 0822507188)
- *From Peanut to Peanut Butter* (ISBN: 082250944X)
- *From Rock to Road* (ISBN: 0822513919)
- *From Sand to Glass* (ISBN: 0822509458)
- *From Sea to Salt* (ISBN: 0822509466)
- *From Sheep to Sweater* ISBN: 0822507161)
- *From Shoot to Apple* (ISBN: 0822507196)
- *From Tadpole to Frog* (ISBN: 0822503999)
- *From Tree to House* (ISBN: 0822513927)
- *From Tree to Paper* (ISBN: 082250720X)
- *From Tree to Table* (ISBN: 0822509474)
- *From Wax to Crayon* (ISBN: 0822546604)
- *From Wheat to Bread* (ISBN: 0822507153)

Galen and the Gateway to Science (Living History Library) by Jeanne Bendick (Bethlehem Books; ISBN: 1883937752; 2002; 152pp)

Teaching with Toys series (McGraw-Hill Trade; 1995)

- *Teaching Chemistry with Toys: Activities for Grades K-9* (ISBN: 0070647224, 304pp) LG & UG

- *Investigating Solids, Liquids, and Gases with Toys* (ISBN: 0070482357; 283pp) UG

Appendix B: Resource List

Uncle Tungsten: Memories of a Chemical Boyhood by Oliver Sacks (Vintage; ISBN: 0375704043; 2002)

Wallace Carothers and the Story of DuPont Nylon (Unlocking the Secrets of Chemistry) by Ann Graham Gaines (Mitchell Lane; ISBN: 1584150971; 2002; 48pp)

Experiment/Science Fair Books

47 Easy-to-Do Classic Science Experiments by Eugene F. Provenzo and Asterie Baker Provenzo, (Dover Publications; ISBN: 0486258564; 1989; 128pp) Only one chemistry experiment in here, but all other experiments will be enjoyed as well. LG/UG

Adventures with Atoms and Molecules — Chemistry Experiments for Young People, Books I – V (Enslow Publishers, 1998; 82pp)

- Book I — ISBN 07660122247
- Book II — ISBN 076612255
- Book III — ISBN 0766012263
- Book IV — ISBN 0766012271
- Book V — ISBN 0-7660-1228-X

Chemical Magic by Leonard A. Ford (Dover Publications; ISBN: 0486676285;1993; 128pp) "magic" tricks using chemistry

Chemicals by John Farndon (Benchmark Books; ISBN: 0761414665; 32pp)

Chemistry by Antonella Meiani (Lerner Publishing Group; ISBN: 0822500876; 2003; 40pp) Grades 4 – 8

Entertaining Science Experiments with Everyday Objects by Martin Gardner (Dover Publications; ISBN: 0486242013; 1981;

Additional Notes

Additional Notes

127pp) LG (UG) Experiments for concepts in chemistry, geometry, astronomy, mathematics, physics, and more.

Famous Experiments You Can Do (An Experimental Science series book) by Robert Gardner (Franklin Watts; ISBN: 053110883X, 1990; 142pp)

Hands-On Chemistry Experiments with Real Life Applications Vol. 2 (Vol. 1 is about physics) by Norman Herr and James Cunningham (Jossey-Bass; ISBN: 0876282621; 2002; 656pp) grades 8 – 12

Janice VanCleave books

- *Janice VanCleave's Chemistry for Every Kid: 101 Easy Experiments that Really Work* (Wiley; ISBN: 0471620858; 1989; 256pp) UG+

- *Janice VanCleave's A+ Projects in Chemistry : Winning Experiments for Science Fairs and Extra Credit* (Wiley; ISBN: 0471586307; 1993; 240pp) UG+

- *Janice VanCleave's Play and Find Out about Science: Easy Experiments for Young Children* (Wiley; ISBN: 0471129410; 1996; 128pp) LG

- *Janice VanCleave's Microscopes and Magnifying Lenses: Mind-Boggling Chemistry and Biology Experiments You Can Turn into Science Fair Projects* (Wiley; ISBN: 047158956X; 1993; 112pp) UG

- *Janice VanCleave's Molecules* (Wiley; ISBN: 047155054X; 1992; 96pp) UG

- *Janice VanCleave's the Human Body for Every Kid: Easy Activities That Make Learn* (M A C, a Modular

Approach to Chemistry) (Sagebrush Bound; ISBN: 0613966813; 1995) UG

- *Janice VanCleave's A+ Projects: Chemistry & Biology* (Wiley; ISBN: 0471024317; 1993; 464pp) UG+

- *Janice VanCleave's Molecules: Mind-Boggling Experiements You Can Turn into Science Fair Projects* (John Wiley & Sons; ISBN: 047155054X; 1993)

Science and the Bible (3 books) by Dr. Donald DeYoug. (Answers in Genesis; 800-778-3390 or www.answersingenesis.org) all ages; easy set-up; common household items; illustrate laws of nature and Biblical principles

Science Fair Projects: Chemistry by Bob Bennet and Dan Keen (Sterling Pub. Co.; ISBN: 080697771X; 2000; 95pp)

Science Fair Success Using Supermarket Products by Salvatore Tocci (Enslow Publishers; ISBN: 0766012883; 2000; 128pp)

Science Projects About Kitchen Chemistry by Robert Gardner (Enslow Publishers; ISBN: 08949095330; 1999; 128pp)

Test Tubes and Beakers: Chemistry for Young Experimenters by E.H. Coulson, A.E.J. Trinder, and Aaron E. Klein (Doubleday; 1971; 134pp)

Fun and Educational Chemisty Kits

Look for chemistry kits at these vendors.

- Smithsonian, www.smithsonianstore.com/home.asp

- Teacher Source, www.TeacherSource.com

Additional Notes

Additional Notes

- Timberdoodle, www.timberdoodle.com

- Wild Goose Science, www.wildgoosescience.com

- Discover This, www.discoverthis.com

- Everything Science, www.everythingscience.com

- Home Training Tools, www.hometrainingtools.com

Traditional Chemistry Sets

- Skillcraft ChemLab 1100 Chemistry Set (Skilcraft); 1100+ experiments; 9+ yrs.

- Skillcraft ChemLab 550 Chemistry Set (Skilcraft); 550+ experiments; 9+ yrs.

Nontraditional Chemistry Sets

These sets use household items or have a unique focus.

- Chemistry Wiz — Solids, Liquids, & Gases (Norman & Globis); 5+ yrs; solids, liquids, gases, state changes; includes colorful lesson book

- My First Chemistry Kit (UC Berkeley GEMS); multiple activities; 4+ yrs; includes 100x-200x-450x microscope

- Smithsonian Crime Scene Investigators Forensic Science Kit; 9+ yrs; microscope, synthetic blood, lab equipment, forensic science book, more

- Slime Chemistry (Wild Goose Science); 9 activities; 8+ yrs; colloidal and polymeric chemistry

Appendix B: Resource List

- Crash and Burn Chemistry Set (Wild Goose Science); 14 activities; 8+ yrs; chemical and physical reactions; may be hard to find

- After Dinner Science Kit (Wild Goose Science); 21 activities; 8+ yrs; biochemistry, organic chemistry

- Kitchen Chemistry (Wild Goose Science); 21 activities; 8+ yrs; organic chemistry

- Oooh Aaah Chemistry Set (Wild Goose Science); 9 activities; 8+ yrs; molecules; acid, base; reactions; may be hard to find

- Soda Bottle Science Kit (Wild Goose Science); 20 activities; 8+ yrs

- Soda Pop Science; Item #SE-503 @ Discover This; multiple activities; 9+ yrs

- Plastic Science Kit; Item #SE-213 @ Discover This; multiple activities; 9+ yrs; polymers, plastics

Additional Notes

From Apologia Education Ministries (www.highschoolscience.com)

Exploring Creation with Chemistry

Apologia Educational Ministries, Inc., is proud to present the second edition of its *Exploring Creation with Chemistry* course. The first edition, originally published in 1995, was the first science course written by Dr. Jay Wile. It took the homeschooling community by storm and set the stage for the rest of Apologia's courses. The second edition of this award-winning chemistry course is even better. It has several new features that greatly enhance the course.

Additional Notes

In order to be able to understand this text, the student needs to have completed algebra I. This course is designed to be a first-year high school chemistry course and gives the student a rigorous foundation in chemistry, in order to prepare him or her for a college-level course. The course covers significant figures, units, classification, the mole concept, stoichiometry, thermochemistry, thermodynamics, kinetics, acids and bases, redox reactions, solutions, atomic structure, Lewis structures, molecular geometry, the gas laws, and equilibrium.

Students who take and understand this course will be well prepared for a tough university chemistry course.

Eco-Hysteria

In this tape, Dr. Wile uses his development as a scientist to explain why most scientists are not creationists, even though the scientific evidence for creation is so compelling. His frank discussions of indoctrination, discrimination, and bias show quite clearly that most scientists do not reject creationism on the basis of science. If you've ever wondered why evolution is so heavily entrenched in the scientific community, you will want to listen to this tape!

Why I Am a Creationist When So Many Other Scientists Are Not?

The material on this 60-minute audiotape explores the current environmentalist movement in the light of our most accurate scientific knowledge. Using scientific data that relate to global warming, acid rain, overpopulation, air pollution, and the ozone layer, Dr. Wile shows how the current environmental debate does not bear much resemblance to the relevant scientific facts. The majority of the environmental hysteria that exists today is the result of media hype, not scientific reasoning.

Dr. Wile's high school chemistry book would be a wonderful addition if you are schooling older students in chemistry while using CKEC with younger ones. Visit www.highschoolscience.com for more information on these materials or to make a purchase.

appendix C

FOR FURTHER BIOGRAPHICAL STUDY

Biographies

Antoine Lavoisier: Founder of Modern Chemistry (Great Minds of Science) by Lisa Yount (Enslow; ISBN: 0894907859; 1997; 128pp)

Louis Pasteur: Disease Fighter by Linda Wasmer Smith (Enslow; ISBN: 0894907905; 1997; 128pp)

Marie Curie: Discoverer of Radium by Margaret Poynter (Enslow; ISBN: 0894904779; 1994; 128pp)

Marie Curie (History Maker Bios) by Laura Hamilton Waxman (Lerner Publications; 2004; 48pp)

The Mystery of the Periodic Table (Living History Library) by Benjamin Wiker and Jeanne Bendick (Bethlehem Books; ISBN: 188393771X; 2003; 170pp)

Additional Notes

Oxford Portraits in Science series, various authors (Oxford University Press) UG

Linus Pauling: And the Chemistry of Life by Tom Hager (ISBN: 0195139720; 2000; 144pp)

Louis Pasteur and the Hidden World of Microbes by Louise Robbins (ISBN: 0195122275, 2001; 128pp)

Francis Crick and James Watson: And the Building Blocks of Life by Edward Edelson (ISBN: 0195114515; 1998; 110pp)

The Story of Science series by Joy Hakim (author of A History of U.S. series). (Smithsonian Institution Press; 2004; 256pp). These books read like adventure stories, and they are filled with chronological narratives about many scientists and their discoveries.
- *The Story of Science, Book One: Aristotle Leads the Way* (ISBN: 1588341607)
- *The Story of Science, Book Two: Newton at the Center* (ISBN: 1588341615)
- *The Story of Science, Book Three: Einstein Adds a New Dimension.* (ISBN: 1588341623)

Youngfolk's Book of Invention by T.C. Bridges (Little, Brown & Company; 1925)

- Read chapter 4, "Iron, Tin, and Steel," for a story about "Dud" Dudley, Andrew Yarranton, and Richard Reynolds. The chapter is available online: http://www.usgennet.org/usa/topic/preservation/science/inventions/cover.htm

- Read chapter 17, "Electric Light and the Phonograph," for a story about Mr. Edison and how carbon became a key to one of his inventions. The chapter is

Appendix C: For Further Biographical Study

available online: http://www.usgennet.org/usa/topic/preservation/science/inventions/cover.htm

- Read chapter 19, "Balloons and Airships," for a story about gases, Bartolome Lorenzo di Guzmao, Francis Lana, Henry Cavendish, Stephen and Joseph Montgolfier, M. Pilâtre de Rozier, and James Sadler. This chapter is available online at: http://www.usgennet.org/usa/topic/preservation/science/inventions/cover.htm

- Read chapter 22, "From Gunpowder to High Explosives," for a story about Alfred Nobel's work with acids leading to explosives and establishing the annual Nobel Prize. This chapter is available online at: http://www.usgennet.org/usa/topic/preservation/science/inventions/cover.htm

- Read chapter 26, "Radium and the X-Ray," for a story about Marie Curie. The chapter is available online: http://www.usgennet.org/usa/topic/preservation/science/inventions/cover.htm

- Read chapter 27, "The Electric Furnace," for a story about Henri Moissan and his work with carbon. The chapter is available online: http://www.usgennet.org/usa/topic/preservation/science/inventions/cover.htm

Notable Chemists to Research

- Alchemists (precursors to chemists; ca 400-1400)
- Ampere, Andre Marie
- Armstrong, Henry
- Arrhenius, Svante
- Avogadro, Amedeo

Additional Notes

Additional Notes

- Aristotle
- Astbury, W. T.
- Balmer, Johann Jakob
- Beguin, Jean
- Berthelot, Pierre
- Berthollet, Claude
- Berzelius, Jöns
- Black, Joseph
- Boyle, Robert
- Bunsen, Robert Wilhelm
- Cannizzaro, Stanislao
- Carothers, Wallace Hume
- Carver, Jr., George Washington
- Cavendish, Henry
- Celsius, Anders
- Charles, Jacques Alexandre Cesar
- Clarke, Hans Thacher
- Cottrell, Frederick G.
- Crick, Dr. Francis
- Crookes, Sir William
- Cullun, William
- Curie, Marie (husband-wife team)
- Curie, Pierre (husband-wife team)
- Dalton, John
- Davy, Sir Humphry
- Democritus
- Deville, Sainte-Claire
- Dewar, Sir James
- Dioscorides
- Di Salvo, Francis
- Dovereiner, Francis
- Dulong, Pierre
- Dumas, Jean
- Faraday, Michael
- Frankland, Edward
- Franklin, Benjamin

Appendix C: For Further Biographical Study

- Galen
- Gay-Lussac, Joseph
- Geber
- Gerhardt, Charles
- Gibbs, Josiah
- Goldschmidt, Johann
- Graham, Thomas
- Guldberg, Cato
- Hahn, Otto
- Haiyan, Jabir Ibn
- Hales, Stephen
- Hall, Charles
- Hatfield, Robert
- Helmont, Jan van
- Henri-Etienne
- Heroult, Paul
- Hess, Germain Henri
- Hope, Thomas Charles
- Joliet-Curie, Fredrick (husband-wife team)
- Joliet-Curie, Irene (husand-wife team)
- Joule, James Prescott
- Julian, Percy Lavon
- Kekule, Friedrich August
- Klaproth, Martin Heinrich
- Kohlrausch, Friedrich
- Kolbe, Adolf Wilhelm Hermann
- Kolthoff, Izaak Maurits
- Kwolek, Stephanie
- Laurent, Auguste
- Lavoisier, Antoine
- Le Bel, Achille
- Le Chatelier, Henri
- Leclanche, Georges
- Lemery, Nicholas
- Levene, Phoebus
- Lewis, Gilbert Newton

Additional Notes

Additional Notes

- Libby, Willard
- Leibig, Georg
- Liebig, Justus Von
- Lomonosov, Milhail
- Loschmidt, Johann Josef
- Lowry, Thomas Martin
- Lucas, Howard
- Markovnikov, Vladimir Vasilevich
- Martin, Archer
- Martin, Dean Fredrick
- Mendeleev, Dmitri
- Meyer, Julius Lothar
- Miller, Stanley
- Mitscherlich, Eilhardt
- Morley, Edward
- Moseley, Henry
- Nernst, Hermann
- Newlands, John Alexander Reina
- Nobel, Alfred
- Noyes, Arthur
- Ohm, Georg Simon
- Ostwald, Wilhelm
- Paracelsus, Philippus
- Patterson, Clair Cameron
- Pauling, Linus
- Perkin, William Henry
- Pettenkofer, Max Von
- Priestley, Joseph
- Proust, Joseph-Louis
- Prout, William
- Ramsay, William
- Raoul, Francois
- Richter, Jeremias Benjamin
- Roentgen, Wilhelm Conrad
- Rouxel, Jean
- Rutherford, Daniel

Appendix C: For Further Biographical Study

- Scheele, Karl Wilhelm
- Schonbein, Christian
- Schrodinger, Erwin
- Seaborg, Glenn
- Soddy, Fredrick
- Solvay, Ernest
- Stahl, Georg
- Stas, Jean Servais
- Stefan, Josef
- Stock, Alfred Eduard
- Strassman, Fritz
- Thomson, Sir Benjamin
- Turgot, Anne-Robert-Jacque
- Urey, Harold
- Waage, Peter
- Willstatter, Richard
- Wohler, Friedrich
- Wollaston, William
- Wrinch, Dorothy
- Wurtz, Charles-Adolphe
- Zewail, Ahmed

Additional Notes

Answer Key
Unit One Wrap-Up

1. Chemistry is the structured and formal study of _____.
    a. medicine
    b. matter
    c. baseball

2. A _____ is a specially trained scientist that studies and works with matter.
    a. chemist
    b. veterinarian
    c. biologist

3. Organic chemistry is the study of matter that contains a substance called _____.
    a. dog food
    b. carbon
    c. oxygen

4. When chemists study the matter of living things, it is called _____.
    a. gardening
    b. physical chemistry
    c. biochemistry

Directions to Teachers
Correct answer is bold.

5. A _____ is a piece of scientific glassware that is shaped similar to a drinking glass, holds liquids, can be heated, provides some measuring, and has a spout for pouring.
   a. beaker
   b. salt shaker
   c. flask

6. Various pieces of glassware can be connected together allowing the flow of liquids and gases from one container to another by using a _____.
   a. garden hose
   b. glass tubing
   c. pipette

7. A _____ allows the easy collection of liquids poured from a container and then passes some portion of the liquid through to a container with a smaller top opening.
   a. pie pan
   b. beaker
   c. funnel

8. Chemists use a long cylinder with measurements marked on its side to measure liquid. It is called a _____.
   a. graduated cylinder
   b. tin can
   c. Erlenmeyer flask

9. An easy way to recognize matter is that it has _____ and takes up space.
   a. a number
   b. money
   c. weight

Answer Key: Unit One Wrap-Up

10. Everything in this physical world is either energy or _____.
    a. lazy
    b. atoms
    c. matter

11. All matter can exist in three different states: _____, _____, or _____.
    a. animal, mineral, vegetable
    b. solid, liquid, gas
    c. proton, neutron, electron

12. There are some special characteristics that we can use to identify matter — and in a way, taste is one of them. These are called _____ of matter by chemists.
    a. behaviors
    b. properties
    c. mysteries

13. When matter is made of one or more of the same kind of atoms, it is made of a single _____.
    a. proton
    b. element
    c. color

14. When matter is made of more than one type of atom, it is called a _____.
    a. goofy matter
    b. compound
    c. molecule

15. There are only _____ naturally occurring elements.
    a. 144
    b. 92
    c. 5

16. An element is the purest form of _____ that exists.
    a. ice cream
    b. energy
    c. matter

17. _____ made all of the naturally occurring elements.
    a. Chemists
    b. God
    c. The army

18. When matter is made of more than one element, it must be one of two things: _____ or _____.
    a. a big mistake, an accident
    b. a molecule, an atom
    c. a mixture, a compound

19. When two or more pure compounds physically combine together (like sand and salt), we have a _____.
    a. problem
    b. compound
    c. mixture

20. A _____ is made up of two or more elements. These elements are chemically combined together to form a new substance.

   a. compound
   b. liquid
   c. mixture

Answer Key
Unit Two Wrap-Up

Directions to Teachers
Correct answer is bold.

1. The _____ is the smallest piece of an element you can have.
   a. atom
   b. molecule
   c. bread crumb

2. The region in the center of the atom is the _____.
   a. core
   b. infield
   c. nuclear region

3. The outer region of the atom is called the _____.
   a. extranuclear region
   b. scary place
   c. molecule

4. Inside the nucleus of the atom, there are two types of particles. One type of particle is called _____ and the other type of particle is called _____.
   a. dust, dirt
   b. neutron, proton
   c. proton, electron

5. The protons carry a _____ charge.
   a. negative
   b. battery
   c. positive

6. The number of electrons is _____ the number of protons when the atom is in its uncharged state.
   a. equal to
   b. greater than
   c. trying to count

7. Each of the elements has a number assigned to it called an _____.
   a. atomic clock
   b. atomic fireball
   c. atomic number

8. The atomic number is equal to the number of _____ in one atom of the element.
   a. protons
   b. neutrons
   c. jelly beans

9. The number of protons (the atomic number) is what makes an element _____.
   a. unique
   b. expensive
   c. atomic

10. Atoms that are missing electrons or have extra electrons are called _____.
    a. messed up
    b. ions
    c. protons

Answer Key: Unit Two Wrap-Up

11. Electrons have almost no _____.
    a. charge
    b. money
    c. weight

12. The mass number of the atom comes almost entirely from the mass of the _____ and the mass of the _____.
    a. shell zone, electrons
    b. beans, hotdogs
    c. protons, neutrons

13. Using various _____, scientists have determined the atomic mass of every element.
    a. scientific instruments
    b. good guesses
    c. dangerous experiments

14. Information about the atomic mass and atomic number of elements is presented in a table called the _____.
    a. scientist's dictionary
    b. crossword puzzle
    c. periodic table

15. The periodic table of the elements is arranged according to the elements' _____.
    a. birth date
    b. atomic weight
    c. atomic number

16. Each box in the periodic table contains atomic _____, atomic _____, and chemical _____ for each element.
    a. weight, number, symbol
    b. fireball, energy, symbol
    c. energy, weight, symbol

17. The far right side of the periodic table contains a family called the _____ gases.
    a. important
    b. explosive
    c. noble

18. A _____ is defined as two or more atoms joined together.
    a. molecule
    b. chocolate chip cookie
    c. proton

19. H_2O and O_2 are examples of _____ molecules.
    a. small
    b. large
    c. unknown

20. We know that atoms of the same _____ can come together and atoms of different _____ can come together as well to form molecules.
    a. weight, weights
    b. team, teams
    c. element, elements

Answer Key
Unit Three Wrap-Up

Directions to Teachers
Correct answer is bold.

1. A _____ is a very strong force between atoms that holds them together.
   - **a. chemical bond**
   - b. light saber
   - c. nuclear particle

2. A(n) _____ bond occurs when one or more electrons from one atom are transferred to another atom.
   - a. covalent
   - **b. ionic**
   - c. special

3. There are actually _____ different types of chemicals bonds
   - a. two
   - b. hundreds of
   - **c. five**

4. Electrons in one atom are attracted to the _____ in another atom and this attractive electrical force forms a bond.
   - a. neutrons
   - **b. protons**
   - c. food

5. The bond between Na and Cl that holds the NaCl compound together is _____ bond.
   a. an ionic
   b. a bionic
   c. a covalent

6. In the case of covalent bonds, the electrons are merely _____, and not given away.
   a. sold
   b. shared
   c. destroyed

7. Two chlorine atoms bond by sharing _____ electrons between them.
   a. two
   b. four
   c. a dozen

8. When one chlorine atom is covalently bonded to another chlorine atom, this forms a _____ of chlorine.
   a. mass
   b. molecule
   c. bottle

9. A _____ tells us what chemicals make up the compound.
   a. telephone message
   b. chemical formula
   c. chemical reaction

10. Chemical _____ are used in formulas to represent the elements.
    a. compounds
    b. symbols
    c. factories

Answer Key: Unit Three Wrap-Up

11. The formula H_2O means that there are _____ atom(s) of hydrogen bonded with _____ atom(s) of oxygen.
    a. too many, too few
    b. one, two
    c. two, one

12. The chemist signifies two molecules of H_2O by writing a 2 in _____ of the formula.
    a. front
    b. back
    c. parentheses

13. Table salt has the chemical name of _____.
    a. sodium nitrate
    b. sodium chloride
    c. Benjamin Franklin

14. Remember, _____ created the elements and their chemical properties.
    a. scientists
    b. squirrels
    c. God

15. _____ and other scientists have developed a system of naming things in order to work with them.
    a. Chemists
    b. Librarians
    c. Hockey teams

16. Sodium chloride is an example of a type of compound, called a _____ compound.
    a. scarry
    b. binary
    c. fundamental

17. The actual event when the chemicals come together and bond is called a _____.
    a. birthday party
    b. chemical reaction
    c. chemical equation

18. A chemical _____ is one of many things that can result from chemical reactions.
    a. bond
    b. nucleus
    c. clearance sale

19. The _____ are the substances we begin with in a reaction.
    a. products
    b. dirty socks
    c. reactants

20. The _____ are what remain after the reaction takes place.
    a. products
    b. leftovers
    c. reactants

21. The best definition for an acid is that it can donate or give away a _____ in a reaction.
    a. prize
    b. proton
    c. neutron

Answer Key: Unit Three Wrap-Up

22. Acids corrode, or eat away, _____.
    a. metals
    b. plastics
    c. ice cream sandwiches

23. Acids react with another type of compound called _____.
    a. bases
    b. baseballs
    c. mixtures

24. The definition of _____ is an atom with a charge (+ or -).
    a. acid
    b. ion
    c. fun

25. Bases are _____ to the touch.
    a. slippery
    b. rough
    c. hot

26. Bases _____ hydrogen ions in a reaction.
    a. lose
    b. gain
    c. think about

27. The oceans of the world are filled with _____.
    a. monsters
    b. salt
    c. acid

28. Tin fluoride (SnF$_2$) is a salt made in the laboratory by chemists and is used in toothpaste to _____.

    a. prevent cavities
    b. cause cavities
    c. freshen breath

29. _____ can have sodium chloride, as well as other types of salts that make the organism function properly.

    a. Expensive clothes
    b. Fossil rocks
    c. Living things

30. A salt called _____ is found in chalk and limestone.

    a. calcium carbonate
    b. table salt
    c. sodium chloride

Answer Key
Unit Four Wrap-Up

Directions to Teachers
Correct answer is bold.

1. Molecules in solids, liquids, or gases are always in _____.
   a. motion
   b. trouble
   c. atomic chaos

2. Any kind of matter that has a definite shape and definite volume is a _____.
   a. gas
   b. solid
   c. puzzle

3. In liquids, the _____ move much more often because they have more energy.
   a. molecules
   b. protons
   c. bugs

4. Liquids have an indefinite _____ and a definite _____.
   a. volume, shape
   b. problem, solution
   c. shape, volume

5. Molecules move more when they have more _____.
   a. space
   b. money
   c. energy

6. The molecules in a gas have a lot of _____.
   a. volume
   b. energy
   c. fun

7. _____ tend to spread out and don't stay in one place very long.
   a. Gases
   b. Cats
   c. Solids

8. Gas laws and other laws in chemistry are an example of the order that God has _____ in the physical world of matter.
   a. created
   b. learned
   c. forgotten

9. _____ is a word that is used to mean the amount of force that you apply to a specific area.
   a. Pressure
   b. Stress
   c. Punch

10. Boyle's law says if the pressure is _____, the volume will decrease.
    a. decreased
    b. increased
    c. released

Answer Key: Unit Four Wrap-Up

11. Charles's law says if the temperature is _____, the volume will increase.
    a. decreased
    b. increased
    c. cold

12. Gas molecules really do obey the _____.
    a. speed limit
    b. gas laws
    c. ten commandments

13. The difference between solids, liquids, and gases is really the difference in the amount of _____ the molecules have.
    a. money
    b. power
    c. energy

14. Heat is _____ that can be put into matter.
    a. temperature
    b. energy
    c. wasted

15. The temperature at which a solid melts is called the _____ point.
    a. final
    b. important
    c. melting

16. The temperature at which a liquid freezes is called the _____ point.
    a. freezing
    b. extreme
    c. good

17. The temperature at which a liquid becomes a gas is called the _____ point.
    a. gaseous
    b. boiling point
    c. your

18. A _____ means that two or more substances are mixed very well together so that all the different atoms and molecules are evenly distributed.
    a. solution
    b. mess
    c. compound

19. There are two types of ingredients in a solution: the _____ and the _____.
    a. important, unimportant
    b. solvent, solute
    c. liquid, solid

20. Soft drinks are a _____ / _____ / _____ solution.
    a. solid, liquid, gas
    b. gas, gas, gas
    c. liquid, liquid, gas

Answer Key
Unit Five Wrap-Up

Directions to Teachers
Correct answer is bold.

1. _____ are a family of compounds that are made of various combinations and amounts of the element hydrogen and the element carbon.
    a. **Hydrocarbons**
    b. Hydroxyl groups
    c. Cheeseburgers

2. Hydrocarbons make up a type of chemistry called _____.
    a. hydrogen chemistry
    b. **organic chemistry**
    c. complicated chemistry

3. The simplest hydrocarbon compound is _____ gas with the formula of CH_4.
    a. mostly
    b. **methane**
    c. propane

4. Carbon atoms have _____ available bonding sites.
    a. no
    b. 2
    c. **4**

5. For the _____ group, the covalent bonds between the carbon atoms are all single covalent bonds.
    a. alkyne
    b. alkane
    c. al capone

6. Alkanes, alkenes, and alkynes are the three major types of hydrocarbons made of only _____ atoms and _____ atoms.
    a. carbon, hydrogen
    b. carbon, oxygen
    c. big, little

7. The alkane compounds have an _____ suffix at the end.
    a. -yne
    b. -ing
    c. -ane

8. The alkenes are like alkanes except they have at least one _____ bond between carbon atoms.
    a. double
    b. triple
    c. superglue

9. The simplest alkene is _____ with a chemical formula of C_2H_4.
    a. ethene
    b. propene
    c. hot chocolate

Answer Key: Unit Five Wrap-Up

10. The alkynes are like the alkanes and the alkenes in that they are made up entirely of _____ and _____.

    a. carbon, hydrogen
    b. carbon, sodium
    c. chocolate, vanilla

11. _____ use three of the four covalent bonding sites on a carbon atom just to bond two carbons together.

    a. Alkynes
    b. Alkanes
    c. Tuna salads

12. The suffix _____ is used in the name of the triple-bonded alkynes.

    a. -yne
    b. -ene
    c. -ing

13. Organic chemistry compounds are divided into hydrocarbons and hydrocarbon _____.

    a. derivatives
    b. lunches
    c. molecules

14. _____ are formed when an OH group is substituted for one of the hydrogen atoms on the hydrocarbon.

    a. Esters
    b. Alcohols
    c. Giant cats

15. Esters are another hydrocarbon _____.
    a. problem
    b. derivative
    c. particle

16. Esters are formed by a reaction of _____ and _____.
    a. acids, alcohols
    b. acids, bases
    c. mustard, pickles

17. Depending on the _____ and _____ used in the reaction, a variety of esters can be made.
    a. time, temperature
    b. acid, base
    c. acid, alcohol

18. Esters are found naturally in many _____.
    a. plants
    b. starships
    c. bacteria

19. Esters are recognizable because of the presence of the _____.
    a. free food
    b. ester group
    c. chemical reaction

20. More bonds between carbon atoms mean more _____.
    a. fun
    b. strength
    c. carbons

Answer Key: Unit Five Wrap-Up

21. Nucleic acids are _____ molecules.
    a. inorganic
    b. mixed up
    c. information

22. Depending on the sequence of _____, different proteins are made for different purposes.
    a. silverware
    b. amino acids
    c. carbohydrate molecules

23. The large _____ molecule is called polysaccharide.
    a. hydrogen
    b. carbohydrate
    c. candy bar

24. Monosaccharides are sugars such as _____ and _____
    a. glucose, fructose
    b. garden hose, radiator hose
    c. fat, protein

25. Fat cells allow animals to store _____ for later use.
    a. heat
    b. energy
    c. sun tan lotion

INDEX

A

The Absent Minded Professor, 67
Acetic acid, 128
Acid, 131–135
    ascorbic, 134
    citric, 110, 134
    definition of, 261
    in ester formation, 241
    experiment on, 133–135, 145–147
    formic, 135
    hydrochloric, 132
    nucleic, 248
    phosphoric, 134
    salicylic, 134
Acids, amino, 248
Actinium, 282
Air, 38, 125, 169
Alcohol(s), 233–238
    definition of, 233, 261
    in ester formation, 241
    experiment on, 235–238
    isopropyl, 235–238
Alka-Seltzer, 109–110
Alkane, 217–218, 261
Alkanes, 210, 215
Alkenes, 210, 221–224, 261
Alkynes, 210, 227–230, 261
Aluminum, 182, 282
Americium, 282
Amino acids, 248
Ammonium hydroxide, 138, 140
Antacid, 144
Antimony, 282
Apparatus, 14, 261. *See also* Equipment
Argon, 77, 282
Arsenic, 282
Ascorbic acid, 134
Asphalt, 209–210
Astatine, 282

Atomic mass, 69–71
Atomic number, 63–66, 262
Atoms, 21, 55–60
    charge of, 57, 64
    definition of, 261
    models of, 58–60
    particles in, 56–58

B
Baking soda, 110, 128
Balance, 17
Barium, 282
Bases, 131, 137–140, 262
Beaker, 15
Beer, 234
Berkelium, 282
Beryllium, 282
Binary, 120, 262
Binary compound, 120, 262
Biochemistry, 6, 247–252, 262
Biology, definition of, 6, 262
Bismuth, 282
Blood, 84
Body, human, elements in, 33
Bohrium, 282
Boiling point, 22, 182–183, 262
Bond(s), chemical, 99–103
    covalent, 107–110, 263
    definition of, 99, 262
    and electrons, 83–84, 99–100, 107–108
    experiment on, 109–110
    ionic, 99–100, 264
    ionic vs. covalent, 144
    and reactions, 125
Books, reference, 287–309
Boron, 282
Boyle's law, 176
Brain, 144
Bromine, 282

Butane, 216
Butter, 10

C
Cadmium, 282
Calcium, 43, 172, 282
Calcium carbonate, 144
Calcium hydroxide, 138
Californium, 282
Carbohydrates, 248–249
Carbon
    atomic number of, 63
    atomic structure of, 56
    definition of, 262
    as diamonds, 179
    symbol for, 282
    uses of, 6
Carbon dioxide, 110, 128
Cerium, 282
Cesium, 282
Chadwick, James, 56
Chain, 208
Chalk, 144
Charles, Jaques, 176
Charles's law, 176, 177–179
Chemical nomenclature, 119–123
Chemical properties, 22, 23
Chemist(s), 5, 263
    famous, 309–312
Chemistry
    danger in, 13
    definition of, 5, 263
    inorganic, 6
    organic, 6, 207–252, 265
    reference books on, 287–309
Chlorine, 30
    atomic number of, 64
    and covalent bonding, 107–108

Index

and ionic bonding, 100
properties of, 217
symbol for, 282
Chromium, 282
Citric acid, 110, 134
Cleaners, 140
Coal, 210
Cobalt, 282
Color, 22
Compound, 30, 37–38
   binary, 120, 262
   definition of, 263
   experiment on, 40–43
   naming of, 119–123
   organic, 207, 265
Contamination, 24
Cookies, 67
Copper, 238, 282
Covalent bonds. *See under* Bonds
Crayons, 243
Creation, 6–7, 51
Curium, 282

D

Darmstadtium, 282
Diamonds, 179
Diesel fuel, 209
Digestion, 144
Dilution, 190, 263
DNA, 248
Dubnium, 282
Dysprosium, 282

E

Eggs, 145–147
Einsteinium, 282
Electrical charge, of atoms, 57, 64
Electrons, 56–57
   and atomic mass, 69
   and bonds, 83–84, 99–100
   and covalent bonds, 107–108
   definition of, 263
   sharing of, 107–108
   shells, 56–57, 76–77
Element cards, 32–33, 72–73, 115–116, 171–172
Elements, 29–34
   abbreviations of, 282–283
   in air, 38
   definition of, 263
   in human body, 33
   in water, 30
Energy, 21, 263
Equation, 126, 263
Equipment, 14–17
Erbium, 282
Erlenmyer flask, 15
Esters, 241–244, 263
Ethane, 209, 216
Ethanol, 234
Ethene, 221
Ethyl ethanoate, 242
Europium, 282
Experiments
   on acid, 133–135, 145–147
   on alcohol, 235–238
   on alkanes, 217–218
   on alkenes, 223–224
   on alkynes, 229–230
   on bases, 139–140
   on bonds, 109–110
   on Charles's law, 177–179
   on chemical reactions, 128–129
   on filtration, 24–27, 101–103
   on freezing point, 184–186, 235–238
   on hydrocarbons, 211–212, 217–218, 223–224

on macromolecules, 249
on matter, 8–10
on measurement, 17–18
on mixtures and compounds, 40–43
on naming compounds, 121–123
on solutions, 191–194
on volume, 164–166
Extranuclear region, 55, 56, 263

F
Fats, 249
Fermium, 282
Ferric oxide, 23
Filtration, 24–27, 101–103
Fingernail polish, 242
Flask, 15
Fluorine, 282
Formic acid, 135
Formulas, 113–116, 262
Francium, 282
Free, definition of, 263
Freezing point, 182, 184–186
Fructose, 249
Fruit, 242
Funnel, 16

G
Gadolinium, 282
Gallium, 282
Gas, 22, 169–170
    definition of, 263
    in mixtures, 39
Gas laws, 175–179
Gasoline, 209
Germanium, 282
Glass, 140, 218
Glass tubing, 15
Glasses, safety, 14, 266

Glucose, 84, 191, 249
Gold, 60, 282
Goldstein, Eugene, 56
Graduated cylinder, 16
Greek, 212
Groups, 77–78
Gunpowder, 144

H
Hafnium, 282
Hair coloring, 140
Hassium, 282
Headaches, 134
Heart, 172
Heat, 127
Helium, 77, 169–170, 282
Hemoglobin, 84
Hexane, 216
Holmium, 282
Human body
    elements in, 33
    minerals in, 43
    salt in, 143
Hydrocarbons, 207–212
    definition of, 207, 208, 264
    examples of, 209–210
    experiments on, 211–212, 217–218, 223–224
    liquid, 211–212
Hydrochloric acid, 132, 144
Hydrogen
    and covalent bonding, 108
    Greek roots of word, 212
    symbol for, 282

I
Ice, 22, 27
Indium, 282
Ingredients, 8–9
Inorganic chemistry, 6, 264

Index

International Union of Pure and Applied Chemistry (IUPAC), 119
Interpolate, 16, 264
Intravenous medication, 191
Iodine, 282
Ionic bonds. *See under* Bonds
Ions, 64, 100, 131–132
    definition of, 264
Iridium, 282
Iron, 22, 282
    boiling point of, 183
    melting point of, 182
Isopropyl alcohol, 235–238
Isotope, 70
IV medication, 191

J
Jet fuel, 209

K
Kelvin temperature, 176
Kerosene, 209
Krypton, 77, 282

L
Lab coat, 14, 264
Laboratories, 13–15
Lanthanum, 282
Latin, 216
Lawrencium, 282
Lead, 218, 282
Lewis, Jerry, 67
Limestone, 144
Liquids, 162–163, 264
Lithium, 58–59, 282
Lithium hydroxide, 138
Liver, 234
Lutetium, 282

M
MacMurray, Fred, 67
Macromolecules, 250–252
Magnesium, 282
Manganese, 282
Mass, atomic. *See* Atomic mass
Matter, 21–23
    definition of, 5, 21, 264
    examples of, 5
    experiment on, 8–10
    states of, 22
Measurement, 16–18
Medicine, 6
Meiternium, 282
Melting point, 22, 182, 264
Mendelevium, 282
Mercury
    atomic structure of, 56
    symbol for, 282
Methane, 208–209, 216, 233
Methanol, 233–234
Minerals, in body, 43
Mixture, 37–39
    definition of, 264
    experiment on, 40–43
    types of, 39
M&M's, 67
Models
    of atoms, 58–60
    of hydrocarbons, 211–212, 217–218, 223–224
    of molecules, 85–86
Molecules, 83–86
    definition of, 264
    in gases, 169
    models of, 85–86
Molybdenum, 282
Monosaccharides, 249, 265
Motor oil, 211–212

N

Names, chemical
    of compounds, 119–123
    definition of, 262
Natural gas, 209
Neon, 77, 230, 282
Neptunium, 282
Neutron, 55, 57
    and atomic weight, 70
    definition of, 265
    and isotopes, 70
Nickel, 238, 282
Niobium, 282
Nitrogen, 29, 63, 283
Nobelium, 283
Noble gases, 77
Nomenclature, chemical,
    119–123, 262
Nucleic acids, 248
Nucleus, 55, 265
The Nutty Professor, 67

O

Oceans, 143, 194
Octane, 216
OH group, 233–234, 265
Oil, crude, 209
Organic chemistry, 6, 207–252, 265
Organic compounds, 207, 265
Osmium, 283
Oxygen, 30, 84, 283

P

Palladium, 283
Particle physicists, 73
Paving, of roads, 209–210
Pentane, 216
Perfume, 244
Periodic law, 76, 265
Periodic table, 75–81, 284
    definition of, 265
    exercise on use of, 79–81
    groups in, 77–78
    invention of, 75
    organization of, 76
    periods in, 76–77
Periods, 76–77
Petroleum, 209
Petroleum jelly, 211–212
Phosphoric acid, 134
Phosphorous, 43, 283
Physical properties, 22, 265
Physics, 21, 265
Pipette, 16
Platinum, 283
Plutonium, 283
Poison, 13
Poison ivy, 252
Polonium, 283
Polyester, 242
Polysaccharides, 249, 265
Potassium, 283
Potassium chloride, 144
Potassium hydroxide, 138, 144
Potassium nitrate, 144
Praseodymium, 283
Prefixes, 228
Pressure, 175
Products, 126, 265
Promethium, 283
Propane, 215, 216
Propene, 222
Properties
    chemical, 22, 23
    definition of, 262
    physical, 22
Propyne, 227–230
Protactinium, 283

Index

Proteins, 248
Proton, 55, 56, 57
   in acids and bases, 137
   and atomic mass, 69
   and bonds, 99
   definition of, 265
Purification, of water, 104

R
Radium, 283
Radon, 77, 283
Reactants, 126, 266
Reactions, chemical, 125–129
   definition of, 263
   experiment on, 128–129
Reference materials, 287–309
Rhenium, 283
Rhodium, 283
Ring, 208
RNA, 248
Roads, 209–210
Roofing, 209–210
Rubidium, 283
Rust, 23, 126–127
Ruthenium, 283
Rutherfordium, 283

S
Safety glasses, 14, 266
Salicylic acid, 134
Salt(s), 24, 30, 38, 143–147
   definition of, 266
   formation of, 144
   in human body, 143
   ionic bond in, 100
   in ocean, 143
   in water, and freezing point, 184–186
Samarium, 283
Sand, 24, 38, 140
Saturation, 190, 266
Scale. *See* Balance
Scandium, 283
Seaborgium, 283
Selenium, 283
Shells, 56–57, 76–77, 100, 107–108
Silicon, 283
Silicon dioxide, 38
Silver, 283
Smell, 22, 244
Snakes, 129
Soda, 190
Sodium, 30
   atomic number of, 64
   and ionic bonding, 100
   properties of, 217
   symbol for, 283
Sodium acetate, 128
Sodium bicarbonate, 110, 128
Sodium chloride. *See* Salt
Sodium hydroxide, 137–138, 140
Sodium nitrate, 144
Soli, definition of, 266
Solids, 161–162
Solutions, 189–194
   definition of, 266
   dilute, 190
   experiment on, 191–194
   saturated, 190
Solvent, 189–194, 266
State change, 181–186, 266
States, of matter, 22, 161–194, 266
Stomach acid, 144
Strontium, 283
Subscript, 113
Sucrose, 114
Suffixes, 228
Sugar, 84, 114, 249

Sulfur, 283

T
Tantalum, 283
Taste, 22
Technetium, 283
Tellurium, 283
Temperature, and gas laws, 176
Terbium, 283
Test tube, 15
Thallium, 283
Thermometer, 17
Thorium, 283
Thulium, 283
Tin, 283
Titanium, 283
Toothpaste, 143
Tubing, glass, 15
Tungsten, 283

U
Ununbium, 283
Ununhexium, 283
Ununium, 283
Ununoctium, 283
Ununpentium, 283
Ununquadium, 283
Ununseptium, 283

Ununtrium, 283
Uranium, 283
Urushiol, 252

V
Vanadium, 283
Vinegar, 128
Volume, 163–166

W
Water, 22
    boiling point of, 183
    elements in, 30
    molecules, 83
    purification of, 104
Word search, on filtration, 27

X
Xenon, 77, 283

Y
Ytterbium, 283
Yttrium, 283

Z
Zinc, 283
Zirconium, 283

About the Authors

Robert W. Ridlon, Jr., is a consultant for a systems development firm and an adjunct faculty member at Southwestern Illinois College, teaching courses in information systems theory. He earned a bachelor of arts degree in biological sciences from Indiana University and a master of science degree in information resource management from the Air Force Institute of Technology.

Elizabeth J. Ridlon is an adjunct faculty member at Southwestern Illinois College where she teaches biological sciences. She earned a bachelor of science degree in microbiology from Indiana University, a master of arts degree in biology from the University of Nebraska, and a secondary teaching certificate from Southern Illinois University.

The Ridlons are involved members of their church and committed to God's message of Truth. They have one son, Robert (in graduate school); a daughter-in-law, Crystal; and two grandsons. The Ridlons have visited and explored 17 countries on four continents and have written two creation science books, including *Creation or Evolution: Does It Matter?*

Also Available from Bright Ideas Press...

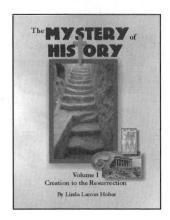 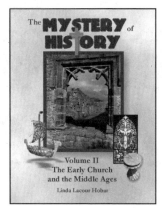 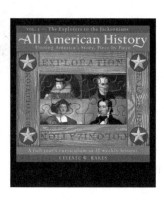 

The Mystery of History Volumes I & II by Linda Hobar

This award-winning series provides a historically accurate, Bible-centered approach to learning history. The completely chronological lessons shed new light on who walked the earth when, as well as on where important Bible figures fit into secular history. Grades 4 – 8, yet easily adaptable.

- Volume I: Creation to the Resurrection — ISBN: 1-892427-04-4
- Volume II: The Early Church & the Middle Ages — ISBN: 1-892427-06-0

All-American History by Celeste W. Rakes

Containing hundreds of images and dozens of maps, *All-American History* is a complete year's curriculum for students in grades 5 – 8 when combined with the *Student Activity Book* and *Teacher's Guide* (yet adaptable for younger and older students).

There are 32 weekly lessons, and each lesson contains three sections examining the atmosphere in which the event occurred, the event itself, and the impact this event had on the future of America.

- Student Reader — ISBN: 1-892427-12-5
- Student Activity Book — ISBN: 1-892427-11-7
- Teacher's Guide — ISBN: 1-892427-10-9

Christian Kids Explore Biology by Stephanie Redmond

One of Cathy Duffy's 100 Top Picks! Elementary biology that is both classical and hands-on. Conversational style and organized layout makes teaching a pleasure.
ISBN: 1-89242705-2

Christian Kids Explore Earth & Space by Stephanie Redmond

Another exciting book in this award-winning series! Author Stephanie Redmond is back with more great lessons, activities, and ideas.
ISBN: 1-892427-19-2

For ordering information, call 877-492-8081 or visit www.BrightIdeasPress.com.

Bright Ideas Press books are available
online or through your favorite
Christian bookstore or homeschool supplier.

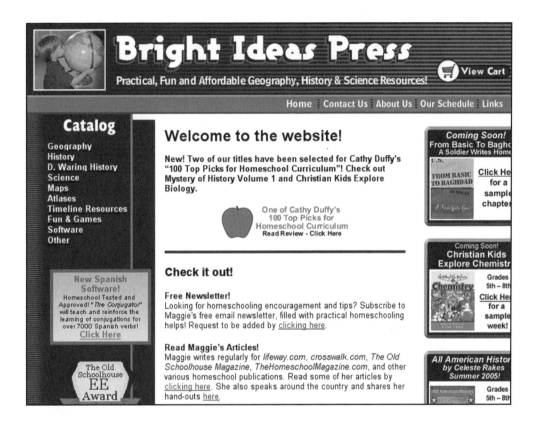

Hey Parents!

Here's a great place to:

Read curriculum reviews
See sample chapters of new books
Sign up for an exciting and useful e-zine
Join our Yahoo groups
Check our homeschool conference schedule
Explore Geography, History, and Science resources
Find great deals on our products!

Secure, online ordering available

www.BrightIdeasPress.com